The Kindness that Kills

The Kindness that Kills

The Churches' Simplistic Response to Complex Social Issues

Edited by

DIGBY C. ANDERSON

First published 1984
SPCK
Holy Trinity Church
Marylebone Road
London NW1 4DU

Copyright © The Social Affairs Unit 1984

ACKNOWLEDGEMENTS

Excerpts from *Understanding Closed Shops: A Christian
Enquiry into Compulsory Trade Union Membership* (CIO
Publishing 1977) are reproduced by kind permission of
the Central Board of Finance of the Church of England.

Excerpts from *Racism in British Society* (CCRJ 1983) are
reproduced by kind permission of the Catholic Commission for Racial Justice.

British Library Cataloguing in Publication Data

The Kindness that kills.
1. Church and social problems
I. Anderson, Digby C.
261.8   HN31

ISBN 0-281-04096-6

Typeset by Pioneer, East Sussex
Printed in Great Britain by
Whitstable Litho Ltd, Whitstable, Kent

Contents

Contents

The Contributors

DR DIGBY ANDERSON is Director of the Social Affairs Unit. His books include *Evaluating Curriculum Proposals, The Ignorance of Social Intervention* and *Health Education in Practice*. He has contributed to *Philosophy of the Social Sciences, Instructional Science, The Journal of Curriculum Studies, Sociology, The Information Design Journal* and *The Journal of Economic Affairs*. He is Editor of the Social Affairs Series on the welfare state 'Agenda for Debate' and the Unit's Research Reports.

LORD HARRIS OF HIGH CROSS is Director-General of the Institute of Economic Affairs. After teaching economics at St Andrews University, he launched the Institute in 1957. Among his most recent writings are *The End of Government, Confessions of a Radical Reactionary* and, with Arthur Seldon, *Overruled on Welfare*.

DR GRAHAM DAWSON taught for eight years in comprehensive schools and is currently Head of Economics at Birkenhead School. He has contributed papers to *Philosophical Quarterly, Philosophy, Economics,* the *Journal of Further and Higher Education* and *The Journal of Economic Affairs*. He is one of the authors of the Social Affairs Unit collection of essays, *The Pied Pipers of Education*.

DR K. B. EVERARD was, until recently, ICI Education and Training Manager. An elder of the United Reformed Church and member of its former Industrial Affairs Advisory Group, he has written, lectured and broadcast on business ethics and contributed to several URC and Methodist publications. He is a governor and honorary lecturer at Luton Industrial College and has contributed to the Social Affairs Unit collection of essays, *Educated for Employment?*

LORD BAUER is Professor Emeritus at the London School of Economics. The author of numerous papers, his books include: *Equality, the Third World and Economic Delusion, Aspects of Nigerian Development, Dissent on Development* and *Indian Economic Policy and Development*.

DR P. A. J. WADDINGTON lectures in Social Psychology at the University of Reading. He was previously lecturer in Sociology at the University of Leeds and has contributed both to sociological and crime and police journals. He is the author of a recent Social Affairs Research Report, *Are the Police Fair?*

JOHN GREENWOOD was Senior Lecturer in Economics at the University of Manchester Institute of Science and Technology and before that lecturer in Economics at Sussex University. He specialized in labour economics, publishing in the *British Journal of Industrial Relations* and *Industrial Relations Journal*. He is currently Chairman and Managing Director of John Williams and Co.

DR DENNIS O'KEEFFE is Senior Lecturer in the Department of Teaching Studies at the Polytechnic of North London. A sociologist and economist by training, he has published papers in the *Journal of Curriculum Studies, Policy Review,* and *Encounter.* His study, *The Sociology of Human Capital,* is in press.

ROBERT MILLER is a consultant to the Institute of Economic Affairs, the London International Financial Futures Exchange and a firm of financial futures brokers. He is the author and co-author of three Institute of Economic Affairs studies: *Exchange Control for Ever?, State Forestry for the Axe* and *What Price Unemployment?*

LADY COX is Director of the Nursing Education Research Unit at Chelsea College, University of London. Her publications include *People in Polytechnics, A Sociology of Medical Practice* and *A Guide to Sociology for Nurses, Midwives and Health Visitors.* The author of many educational papers, she collaborated with John Marks on *The Right to Learn,* and with John Marks and Maciej Pomian-Srzednicki on *Standards in English Schools.*

DR JOHN MARKS is Senior Lecturer in the School of Applied Physics at the Polytechnic of North London. His publications include *Relativity* and *Science and the Making of the Modern World.* He has collaborated with Caroline Cox on many educational papers and books such as *The Right to Learn* and *Standards in English Schools.*

PROFESSOR BRIAN GRIFFITHS is Dean of the City University Business School and former Director of the Centre for Banking and International Finance at the City University. He has served as Economic Adviser to the Canadian Government, as Visiting Economist to the Ministry of Finance and Bank of Mexico, and as a member of the Panel of Academic Consultants to the Bank of England, of which he is a Director. He has written and broadcast extensively in the field of money and finance and also on the theological and ethical aspects of economic life. He is the author of *Morality and the Market Place*.

DR MACIEJ POMIAN-SRZEDNICKI is a Research Fellow at the National Council for Educational Standards. He took a PhD in Sociology at London University, is a member of the Editorial Board of *Religion in Communist Lands* (published by Keston College) and his publications include *Religious Change in Contemporary Poland* (RKP 1982) and *Standards in English Schools*, co-authored with John Marks and Caroline Cox.

ALEXANDER TOMSKY, who was born in Czechoslovakia, is a Researcher at Keston College. He is a specialist on Catholics in Eastern Europe and is a member of the Editorial Board of *Religion in Communist Lands*. He has written articles for numerous papers and journals (in particular *Religion in Communist Lands, Index on Censorship* and *Communio*), and he frequently appears on radio and television.

THE REV. DR WILLIAM ODDIE is a priest-librarian of Pusey House and a fellow of St Cross College, Oxford, and is the Bishop of Oxford's chaplain to post-graduate students at Oxford University. He contributes regular articles on church affairs to *The Daily Telegraph*. His publications include *Dickens and Carlyle: The Question of Influence* (1972), and *What will Happen to God: Feminism and the Future of Christian Belief* (1984).

PROFESSOR DAVID MARTIN is Professor of Sociology at the London School of Economics. He is the author of numerous papers in journals including *Encounter, Daedalus, TLS* and *THES*. His books include *The Breaking of the Image, Dilemmas of Contemporary Religion, A General Theory of Secularisation* and *A Sociology of English Religion*.

RACHEL STEARE is Research Assistant to the Dean at the City University Business School. She was formerly engaged in research and writing on development issues for the UK Committee for UNICEF (United Nations Children's Fund).

Critical Sources

The following Church publications are examined critically. Chapter numbers in brackets refer to their appearance in this book.

1   *Community, Wealth and Taxation,* The Laity Commission 1982. [Chapter 1]

2   Rev. David Moorland OSB, *The Eucharist and Justice,* Infoform for the Catholic Information Office 1980. [Chapter 1]

3   P. Brett and A. Dyson, ed., *Transnational Corporations: Confronting the Issues,* CIO 1983. [Chapter 2]

4   *Work in Life,* Council of Industrial Mission in Hertfordshire and Bedfordshire, Winter 1980, No. 3. [Chapter 2]

5   *Facing the Facts: the UK and South Africa,* Church of England 1982. [Chapter 2]

6   *South Africa and Ourselves,* BCC and CCSA, November 1982. [Chapter 2]

7   *The Churches and the Multinationals – How to Get into the Debate,* Working Paper No. 5, Church of England Synod Board for Social Responsibility Industrial Committee, December 1978. [Chapter 2]

8   R. Stares, *ICI in South Africa,* Christian Concern for South Africa, March 1977. [Chapter 2]

9   B. Rogers, *A Code for Misconduct,* CCSA, 1980. [Chapter 2]

10   R. Stares, *Black Trade Unions in South Africa; The Responsibilities of British Companies,* CCSA October 1977. [Chapter 2]

11   *Populorum Progressio,* 1967. [Chapter 3]

12   *Octogesima Adveniens,* 1971. [Chapter 3]

13   S. Smith, *Race and Crime Statistics,* Race Relations Fieldwork Background Paper No. 4, Church of England General Synod Board for Social Responsibility 1982. [Chapter 4]

14   Church Information Office, *Understanding Closed Shops: A Christian Enquiry into Compulsory Trade Union Membership,* Ludo Press 1977. [Chapter 5]

15   *Racism in British Society,* Catholic Commission for Racial Justice, 1983. [Chapter 6]

16   Bob Jackson, *Government Economic Policy and Concern for My Neighbour,* Grove Pastoral Series No. 12, 1982. [Chapter 7]

17   Paul Brett, *Unemployment and the Future of Work,* Church of England

General Synod Board for Social Responsibility Industrial and Economic Committee, Working Paper 14, 1982. [Chapter 7]

18 *Work or What? A Christian Examination of the Employment Crisis,* an ecumenical group of the BCC, CIO 1977. [Chapter 7]

19 D. Sheppard, *Bias to the Poor,* Hodder & Stoughton 1983. [Chapters 7, 9, 12, 15]

20 *The Cuts and the Wounds — A Christian Response to Cuts in Public Spending,* Internal Economy Group, Thames North Province Church and Society Panel, 1982. [Chapters 8, 15]

21 *Lords Hansard*, especially 8th April 1981 and 29th June 1983. [Chapter 9]

22 Ans J. van der Bent, *Christians and Communists,* World Council of Churches, Geneva 1980. [Chapter 11]

23 *Development Education for the Church of England*, General Synod Board for Social Responsibility, CIO 1983. [Chapter 15]

24 *World Council of Churches Programme on Transnational Corporations Document 2.3.,* WCC, Geneva 1982. [Chapter 15]

Introduction: Under False Colours

Digby Anderson and Ralph Harris

Secular analysis requires secular assessment

Clergy and laity alike are increasingly offered pronouncements on economic and social issues by the Churches and their specialist agencies. They are asked to read and discuss them, pass resolutions about them, take action and urge governments to act. The question is no longer whether the Church should be so preoccupied with socio-economic issues but whether its preoccupations in print and speeches have been thorough and, above all, helpful, either in assisting its members to understand the issues or in comforting those 'in trouble, sorrow, need, sickness or any other adversity'. Many of the speeches and reports contain little theology and are given over to the repetition of arguments found in secular economic and sociological documents at various levels. Thus the question of their quality is one not only for theologians but for economists and sociologists whose disciplines the church authors pillage so covetously.

There have always been individual Christian controversialists like the 'Red Dean', Dean Inge or Archbishop Temple, but they peddled no common party line. As corporate bodies the Churches spoke rarely and carefully about detailed socio-economic issues. Their analyses of such issues were primarily theological and offered as a basis for individual reflection rather than a call to partisan collective action. Always they were wary of putting their massive moral endorsement directly or indirectly behind ephemeral and controversial postures. So long as that prevailed, few economists and sociologists saw much reason to comment on church publications even when they touched on topics of mutual interest. Now that has all changed. Not only have the publications become more frequent; they are now more specific and deploy more secular arguments — they are more tendentious, more policy oriented, more cast in the moulds of secular ideologies, more associated with lobbies and pressure groups and, most objectionable, they are insistent that their reconditioned 'Social

1

Gospel' is not a possible road but the only road to salvation.

It thus seemed appropriate and timely to ask a number of Christian sociologists, economists and theologians to scrutinize some of the thinking from church sources on economic and social issues. The resulting collection of essays, assembled by the Social Affairs Unit, is divided into two parts. The first examines specific publications which are typical treatments of particular issues, for example, the Encyclical letter *Populorum Progressio*'s discussion of Third World poverty or the Board of Social Responsibility's *Understanding Closed Shops*. Other chapters in Part I examine publications on education, unemployment, investment in South Africa, racism, wealth creation, crime and state welfare.

Part II is less concerned with particular reports and controversies than with three matters common to many of them: the relationship of Christianity with Capitalism, Marxism and 'Christian' Socialism; the shifting relationship of the Church to public issues, away from identification with nation and people and towards the role of critic and lobbyist; and guidance on how to use economic and sociological sources together with an assessment of their current use.

Worrying findings and qualifications

The essays express the differing views of their individual authors, not the views of the Social Affairs Unit. What the contributions reveal, apart from a shared suspicion about fashionable 'progressive' opinion, is a common concern about the manner in which church publications have approached these sensitive topics. As economists and sociologists but also as Christians, the authors are worried about the church publications.

Bluntly, if the Churches are to comment on specific and controversial socio-economic issues, they should work harder at being informed and scrupulously even-handed. Their publications are variously found to be sloppy, ill-thought out, ignorant, one-sided, addicted to secular fashions, uncritical of conventional 'progressive' wisdom, hysterical, unmethodical in the use of sources and evidence, theologically desiccated and, most deplorable, uncharitable to those who disagree. If the first principle of morality is, following Pascal, to work hard at thinking clearly, they could be said to be lacking in moral weight.

We should immediately note some reservations. We have written, for convenience, about 'church' publications. This designation needs qualification. First, the publications whose tendencies we criticize are from *various* Churches and church bodies and have varying standing within them. Some, such as the papal letters, have a precise ecclesiastical standing while others are not endorsed officially. Second, many of the publications are not the 'final word' but interim documents to be followed by debate in, for example, a synod. Thus it may be suggested that the faults we find may not prove as serious as we suggest.

There is truth in this. Certainly bishops, clergy and people *have* offered thoughtful comments on the publications in subsequent debate which have considerably improved on the original publications. We applaud them. Equally certainly there are some churchpeople who understand many of the publications lack authority and treat them accordingly.

But neither of these important facts excuses or compensates for the defects in the publications for the following reasons. First, 'interim' texts such as working party reports can be extremely influential in setting the tone, priorities and alternatives of any such subsequent debate. Second, their influence extends beyond the debating chamber. They are not internal staff papers but national publications which are widely distributed. Third, a text does not cease to have *any* authority simply because its authors disavow a precise ecclesiastical authority. Authority, in the sociological sense, is a quality, unlike power, freely accorded to those above by those below. In this case it is certain that the media, and probably many churchpeople, accord a vague 'church' authority to 'church' documents in spite of the humble disclaimers of their 'church' authors. Thus neither explicit disclaimers of authority nor healthy debate are sufficient to cancel the effects of ignorant and unfair publications.

One concession we readily make, however, to the *specific* publications on which we comment is that they are not alone in their weaknesses. Indeed we chose them not because they were exceptionally bad but because they succinctly exemplified poor arguments in more general currency in texts and discussions. Our complaints while occasioned by them are not ultimately addressed to them. Nor would we object to them as *individual* polemics.

Polemical argument, even tendentious argument need not be a bad thing so long as both sides are put somewhere and not necessarily in the same publication. One simple change would remove many of our objections. If bodies such as the Church of England's Board of Social Responsibility sought to publish two or more views on unemployment, housing or the market economy, they might make a valuable contribution to debate and reflect the lack of authority of the publications better than by offering one 'line'.

But the most important implications are for readers, clergy and laity alike. First they should not feel guilty if they are unenthusiastic about these publications and their rousing calls to quasi-political action and involvement. For if many of the reports receive little authority in the Church, they would receive less from economic or sociological research. Secondly, if Christians do read and discuss them it should be with caution and scepticism. We offer such readers the cautions of our analyses as an inoculation against the prevalent disorders in 'Church' reports on socio-economic affairs.

Particular controversies discussed

The implications discussed above are general. But the chapters of Part I also offer analyses of *particular* socio-economic controversies which are part of the contemporary Church's staple diet of debate. Let us now turn to these in brief summary.

Wealth Creation; Investment in South Africa; The Third World

Dr Graham Dawson examines *Community, Wealth and Taxation* published by the Laity Commission and the Rev. David Morland's *The Eucharist and Justice.* He is concerned with the Commission's unbalanced emphasis on wealth distribution and corresponding lack of interest in wealth production. *Community, Wealth and Taxation* takes for granted that the material world provides a livelihood for the asking. The Commission and David Morland exemplify an ancient heresy which held that matter was evil and wanted little to do with it. Dr Dawson explains why wealth creation is still important and argues against the naive compartmentalization of the spiritual and the material.

4

Dr K. B. Everard examines some twelve publications on multi-nationals and South Africa especially R. Stares' *ICI in South Africa*, CCSA *Black Trade Unions in South Africa* and B. Rogers' *A Code for Misconduct*. His chapter is 'not an apologia for multinationals . . . still less for the South African Government. The issues discussed are the unchristian assumptions that frequently underlie it and the damaging counterproductive consequences that stem from such criticism . . .' He finds that Church critics 'impugn the motives of those who direct business affairs . . . smear the character and ethics of business organizations in general . . . distort the nature of capitalism and the market economy, [and] ignore, disparage or minimize the benefits that multinationals bring . . . The resemblance of some of these reports to Marxist literature is . . . striking.'

Lord Bauer considers four common myths endorsed in the Encyclical *Populorum Progressio* and Pontifical letter *Octogesima Adveniens*. The myths are that: Third World poverty is a result of developed countries' riches; governments act for the common good; therefore politically-initiated income redistribution from rich to poor is necessary; and that this should involve land redistribution. Lord Bauer explains that poverty is caused by many factors, not the misconduct of the rich; that governments have not acted for the common good; that political redistribution may aggravate poverty, not reduce it; and that land and resources are not a crucial factor compared with human attitudes and motivation. The papal letters' treatment of Third World poverty is not the result of hard thinking. It seems to strive for easy popularity by repeating secular myths and legitimizing envy.

Black Crime; The Closed Shop; Racism

Dr P. A. J. Waddington discusses a Board of Social Responsibility paper exemplifying a fashionable view that substantial inner city black crime is largely a myth. Dr Waddington shows how admitted difficulties with criminal statistics have been exploited and abused to suggest that the problem is not black crime but police racialism. Only an *exaggerated, distorted* and *inconsistent* analysis, fuelled by an anti-police prejudice, could fabricate such a conclusion. The result is a drawing of attention away from real inner city problems.

John Greenwood analyzes the Board of Social Responsibility's

Understanding Closed Shops. The revealing title betrays the bias. It casts the problem as understanding closed shops rather than understanding those who are sacked for failure to join them. Its new 'understanding' of closed shops will 'mitigate' 'anxieties'. John Greenwood argues that the booklet employs *secular* arguments in an unquestioning way. A secular understanding of closed shops may be necessary for a moral judgement about them but is not sufficient. Among the inadequacies of the arguments deployed, the worst are reliance on *expediency,* disregard for international comparative data, dubious pseudo-Marxist appeals, and failure to consider the morally 'unacceptable face of trade unionism'.

Dr Dennis O'Keeffe takes issue with the Catholic Commission for Racial Justice's *Racism in British Society.* He finds it confused and lacking proportion in its claims. The preference people may feel for their own race is not the same as institutionalized racism. It is not reasonable to confuse mild prejudice with the kind of hatred and murderous intolerance suggested by the term 'racism'. Moreover, the report is conceptually sloppy. It espouses an absurd cultural relativism in which no judgement is allowed about the superiority or inferiority of different cultures — itself a highly dogmatic cultural judgement! No culture is to be allowed more praise than another. Even 'popular notions' of Christian mission merit a sneer. Its analysis of the causes of racism is poor history and worse sociology, and its confidence in state interference as a method for combating racism is nowhere justified by facts and appears purely ideological. It does a disservice to the people it would claim to help.

Unemployment; Education; Welfare

Robert Miller addresses another Board of Social Responsibility text, *Unemployment and the Future of Work,* and Bob Jackson's *Government Economic Policy and Concern for my Neighbour.* He shares their view that unemployment is *theologically* objectionable but not their conclusion that state intervention is the obvious answer. Miller points out that the prescription, unlike the diagnosis, is not based on theological grounds but on weak, one-sided economic analysis. The authors do not appear to be aware of monetarist critiques of intervention or, even more important, of 'public choice' analyses which show how government failure can outweigh market failure. Indeed 'public choice' arguments accord with a doctrine of original sin which is much more realistic about the fallible human nature of intervening bureaucrats than the special pleading of Mr Jackson and the Board of Social Responsibility.

Lady Cox and Dr John Marks discuss a section from *The Cuts and the Wounds* which enshrines several myths about current education problems. They argue against the myths that resources are unlimited, that more money means higher standards, that expenditure on education is being cut, that more teachers mean better education and that resources should be increased. Not only are these popular cries myths but they deflect Christian attention from its proper concerns. More enduring issues are the failures of comprehensive reorganization, religious education in schools, the ideological corruption of the curriculum, and the future of religious schools.

Lord Harris of High Cross examines the Bishops' misunderstandings about welfare as typified by their contributions to House of Lords Debates and David Sheppard's *Bias to the Poor*. Like other authors he finds economic ignorance, political innocence and lack of interest in cost. They appear not to understand that high expenditure on universal welfare must be paid for by the poor and not just the rich. They show no awareness that the resulting taxes distort incentives to invest and to work. They ignore the economic rule that services supplied 'free' will prove inadequate, that the articulate middle classes will do better than the poor, and that inefficient hospitals, schools and welfare departments will be exploited by trade unions for the benefit of those who work in them.

More general issues

Part II considers more general issues underlying such particular discussions.

Capitalism; Marxism; Christian Socialism; The Secular Church of England

Professor Brian Griffiths challenges Bonino's statement that capitalism is 'definitely anti-Christian' and Schumacher's that the market is the 'institutionalization of individualism and non-responsibility'. There is a long history of the Church's antipathy to the market and from an idealistic view the market is indeed less than ideal. But a more realistic judgement is that capitalism creates wealth efficiently and the Church favours the reduction of poverty. Further, capitalism is one of several alternative social orders and the others are even more problematical.

The divorce between Christ's teaching and capitalism is not obvious since that teaching was directed less at the socio-economic order than at spiritual salvation. If we want specific guidance on the socio-economic order we must turn to the Old Testament which offers considerable support for the market within a religious and ethical ideology. Capitalism is not anti-Christian and nor need its stress on the importance of individual competition and profit be rejected out of hand. The challenge is to incorporate capitalism *within* Christianity.

Dr Mariej Pomian-Srzednicki and Dr Alexander Tomsky challenge van der Bent's argument that Christian dialogue with Marxists can enhance 'human dignity, freedom, creativity and wholeness'. 'Progressive' Christians argue that there is a Christian core behind Marxism's atheism and that Communist institutions are strongly based on the practices and traditions of Christianity or at least congruent with it. Certainly there are some resemblances in the rhetoric on unselfishness and neighbour-liness, but the disagreement about method is fundamental. Marxism, like the sixteenth-century 'progressive' Anabaptists, has its heaven on earth and tries to compel its unfree citizens to love one another. The *imposition* of Christian principles is not Christian nor can it have the desired social effects. Only a Christianity without metaphysics, a Christianity which denies the *freedom* to return or not the divine and neighbourly love, and a Christianity blind to Marxism's militant atheism could contemplate such a dialogue.

The Rev. Dr William Oddie disputes Bishop David Sheppard's view that there is biblical authority to suggest a divine 'Bias to the Poor' on the grounds that the Bishop, like many others, interprets the biblical texts in a questionable way. He then goes on to discuss more general issues of poverty, particularly views that are hostile to riches, that attribute the poverty of some to the riches of others, and that initiate a *social* campaign to 'abolish the rich'.

In espousing such ideas Christian Socialism risks repeating a version of Pelagianism, a notorious heresy.

Professor David Martin's chapter analyzes trends in the Church of England which are another example of dubious thinking about a social issue — the Church's relationship to the nation — and a partial explanation of how the modern Church comes to express the dubious views discussed in earlier chapters. Sections of the Church increasingly think of it as a private bureaucratic association and are suspicious of the special link with *this* land, *this* place, *this* people. 'The Church of fact and history is partly dissolving into a Church of opinions, not so much nourishing personal and corporate devotion' as lobbying for political change.

Sources and Hints on Reading

One problem which emerges in many of the previous chapters is that of balance. At least nine of the chapters express concern that the 'church' authors do not use a *balanced* mix of economic or sociological sources. Balance is an elusive concept and certainly has to be a balance of sources *available*. Rachel Steare's chapter is a discussion of the sources available on many of the issues discussed. It is at once a resource for those who wish to read and write on the issues and a checklist for those reading church publications on socio-economic topics. Readers can now check the socio-economic references of church publications to see if sources have been used selectively.

Using sources fairly is not simply a matter of choosing an equal number from each side. All sorts of problems occur when authors in one discipline 'borrow' ideas and 'facts' from another. These borrowed ideas may not be accepted in their own discipline; they may be controversial or hedged about with reservations. Dr Digby Anderson critically analyzes the borrowings that several reports make. He also looks at how they are mixed with other ingredients — theology, sentimentality, ideology, rhetoric and fact — to produce the composite 'pie' that most reports resemble. Consumers are offered criteria to decide whether the report is a competent mix of different disciplines or another discipline's 'leftovers' minced, spiced with sentiment and 'poorly warmed up'.

Love and the Social Gospel

Our contributors have discussed specific church publications on particular socio-economic issues and some more general matters such as misunderstandings about different social orders like Capitalism, Marxism or 'Christian' Socialism, trends to secularization and the use and abuse of sources. The appeals they make are to rather uninteresting virtues including caution, even-handedness, careful thought, analysis and scepticism.

The reconditioned social gospel which many of the church publications typify, and which we criticize, makes a more dramatic appeal. Its invitation is to a crusade for a new covenant of care ideology and social science. Above the crusaders flutter the banners of compassion, community, liberation and social justice interspersed with those of supposed economic and sociological fact. Not for the crusaders anything as vague as the 'banner of love unfurled' or as traditional as a *considered* theology of man and creation. The enemies are clearly defined by sentiment, secular ideology and the newly found social sciences. All that remains is to join battle with the forces of oppression.

We think differently. The issues are complex. If we reject the crusaders' simplistic picture of them it does not, of course, mean that we too do not subscribe to a 'social gospel' though without the self-righteousness of the crusaders. Certainly the banner of love is broad enough to embrace discrimination as well as enthusiasm. Careless care may hurt the very people its well-meaning exponents claim to help. There is a kindness that kills.

PART I

Church Publications on
Socio-Economic Issues

1

God's Creation, Wealth Creation and the Idle Redistributors

Graham Dawson

Christianity and post-materialism

'If you could not prevent the unequal acquisition of wealth, you could at least attempt to prevent its consolidation into relationships of power and powerlessness by timely attempts at redistribution.'[1]

'. . . all power and possessions come from God and must, therefore, be shared out equally among all.'[2]

The two statements quoted may appear to many people to be entirely reasonable expressions of Christian belief. Yet I shall suggest that if acted upon, they would make people worse off in spiritual as well as material terms. At first sight it may seem that all these statements claim is that as stewards of God's creation we have a duty to ensure everyone receives his 'fair share' of material goods. And surely Christians must believe in fair shares for all. That is true. But the problem with the passages quoted is not so much with what they assert but rather with what they omit. It is taken for granted that the material world provides a livelihood merely for the asking. It is as though God, having created us, owes us a living. Consequently, it is unconsciously assumed that with wealth there are only two things we can, and indeed need to do. First, we can acquire it, and then we can redistribute it. This overlooks the need for the creation of wealth. It appears to be thought that sufficient wealth will always be to hand. There is, therefore, no need to think about creating wealth, since God has already done that for us.

This assumption is at once an expression of an ancient heresy and a modern misapprehension. The heresy is Manicheism, which is the belief that matter is evil, from which it follows that any involvement with the material world, including the extraction of its natural resources and their manufacture into material goods, is corrupting. The modern misapprehension calls itself 'post-

13

materialism'.[3] It is a trend of thought which became prominent in the 1960s among those who believed the affluent nations had solved the problem of wealth-creation once and for all and should now turn their attention to its redistribution. Wresting a living from a hostile or indifferent environment could give way to caring for the deprived and disadvantaged. Industry and commerce could, and indeed should, take a back seat while social work came to the fore. We should abandon economics for sociology. At its most extreme, post-materialism found expression in the student movement, where it gave rise to demands for a permissive morality, on the grounds that the control of desire and inclination had been necessary only under conditions of material want.

Now I do not want to say that the whole post-materialist package is unacceptable. What I do want to suggest is that it presents us with a false dichotomy between the material and the spiritual aspects of life. Exploiting the resources of the earth is not to be opposed to caring for the sick and the needy but is a necessary condition for the execution of all humanitarian tasks. The creation of wealth is, indeed, the most fundamental social service of all. It is no exaggeration to say: charity begins at work. That post-materialists do not appreciate this truism is the reason for seeing them as the inheritors of the Manichean heresy.

Material substance and spiritual meaning

Many people will probably feel that hostility, or at least indifference, to material things is a valid interpretation of the Sermon on the Mount. 'You cannot serve God and mammon' (Matthew 6.24). We are, it seems, faced with a dilemma: we must choose between service to God and the pursuit of material well-being, for the two activities are mutually exclusive. A compromise solution, such as serving God in family and social life, while serving mammon in business or at work, looks to be a makeshift and even cynical device for trying to have the best of this world and the next. Moreover, if God demands total devotion, any division of allegiance amounts to dereliction of duty. Nevertheless, we must, I shall argue, understand the claims of mammon if we are to succeed in serving God.

The first premise of my argument is that orthodox Christian belief has always acknowledged the material basis of man, who is

14

made from 'dust of the ground' (Genesis 2.7). Of course man is not just a material being. But the sense in which he is more than that can easily be misunderstood. A human being is not a union of two discrete and independent things, the body and the soul. For matter is not a substance in its own right, not a self-sufficient entity on a par with the soul. Neither is the soul a ghostly counterpart of, and rival to, the body. Spirit does not oppose matter but rather informs it; the soul is what gives value and meaning to the body.

If we think of a human being as merely a material body, we fail to form a complete picture of him. But the picture is incomplete, not because the human being is made of two complete things, body and soul, but because matter is in itself radically inchoate. Consider an approximate analogy: as you read, you are looking at white paper with black marks on it. That is, however, an inadequate description of the object of your attention, because it picks out the material aspect and quite overlooks the meaning communicated to you by the marks. The difference between a series of marks on paper and a word is an aspect of the more general distinction between matter and spirit. The Word is indeed the paradigm of the spiritual.

One way in which spirit informs and completes matter can be seen by reflecting on the use of material goods as necessary means to the attainment of spiritual or humanitarian ends. For instance, a drug, as a material thing, merely alters the chemical condition of another material thing, the body. But its ultimate significance may be as an agent for the relief of pain or the restoration of physical mobility. The car, so often seen as the symbol of Western decadence and exploitation, provides another example. As a material object a car is without meaning; we can measure it and record its shape but we cannot rationally make judgements about it. To the extent that it becomes an object of judgement, it ceases to be a merely material object. Thus, the fact that a car can do 36 mpg at a steady 56 mph is in itself neither commendable nor blameworthy; it is one or the other only in relation to our aims. We have to balance a desire to minimize petrol costs against, say, the need to save time or carry heavy loads. When we choose a car which offers — for the proposed use — the most satisfactory combination of economy, speed and load capacity, we judge it as a human artefact, that is, as the embodiment of purpose and skill.

And so a car is nothing less than the material manifestation of the desire to earn a living by supplying something that will be of use to other people as they go about their daily lives.

Wealth creation and deprivation

If the above analysis of the distinction between matter and spirit is correct, it has two implications for Christians living in a material world imbued with spiritual meaning. These are: firstly, the creation of material wealth is a necessary, but not a sufficient, means to the attainment of many spiritual and humanitarian ends; and, secondly, it is not sufficient because wealth can never be a valid end in itself. Thus, it is true that we cannot serve God and mammon if they are both construed as ultimate ends of conduct. However, it is also true (and it is a truth which post-materialists are likely to overlook) that we cannot serve God without creating and using mammon. Taking that word in its literal meaning of 'money' will illustrate the point.

A miser who hoards money as though it were intrinsically valuable, as though money were nothing more than a collection of material objects and yet worth having for itself, fails to see that matter must be informed by spirit if it is to become something of value. For money is of value to the extent that it can be exchanged for goods and services which satisfy wants. Not realizing this, the miser serves mammon. The post-materialist also sees money as no more than a set of material objects but, instead of accumulating it, rejects it for that reason. He does not serve mammon but neither can he serve God — except as a hermit. For he has cut himself off from the means to many spiritual ends. This is not a merely hypothetical example, for post-materialism is evident in Christian dealings with the real world.

An almost Manichean distaste for the material world appears to underlie a recent call by a Benedictine monk for the West to turn away from affluence and for the Church to strip away its 'riches both secular and ecclesiastical'.[4] This course of action is urged for the sake of the rich as well as for that of the poor.[5] Yet it is precisely the opposite of what is required if the rich are to help the poor out of their poverty, since the need is to create wealth rather than destroy it.

Part of the problem is the traditionally ambivalent attitude of

Christianity towards the poor. The only reasonable attitude towards involuntary poverty is that it is an evil which ought to be eradicated as quickly and as completely as possible. But there have always been Christians who have seen poverty as a blessing on the grounds that its attendant hardship and insecurity are necessary conditions for a full appreciation of one's dependence on God. If poverty is understood in its common usage of a lack of the means to satisfy the basic wants of food, clothing and shelter, then it is simply not true that the involuntarily poor are more sensible of the spiritual dimension of life. Of course there are people who have been led to God by material adversity. But there are many millions more whose poverty imposes on them a ceaseless striving after the means of subsistence which leaves neither time nor energy for spiritual concerns.[6] So there is no reliable connection between involuntary poverty and religious sensibility: material want may brutalize as readily as it may spiritualize.

Affluence is equally uncertain in its spiritual effects. True, debauchery is most conspicuous when it is subsidized from a high income. And the obsessive pursuit of consumer goods can blind the pursuer to the spiritual significance of human life. But it is no less true that modest affluence and even immense fortune can awaken the religious impulse, the one by conferring freedom from pressing material cares, the other by inspiring gratitude and obligation.

All we can say is that wealth and poverty alike contain dark woods as well as right roads.[7]

Capitalism on the side of the poor

I have argued that involuntary poverty limits opportunities to fulfil purposes without necessarily affording any compensating spiritual purity. The practical question is therefore how to eliminate poverty. The Christian post-materialist is tempted in a dangerous direction: he may urge the redistribution of wealth, perhaps through the revolutionary 'liberation' of the poor.

Redistribution is advocated on the grounds that wealth has been unequally and therefore unjustly acquired.[8] There are at least two confusions in this argument. First, inequality is not the same thing as injustice. If some people make better use than others of their skills, and do so for the general well-being, it would be unjust if everyone were to receive the same rewards. Just deserts are not the same as equal shares. The Parable of the Talents is of course an illustration of this point (Matthew 25.14-30).

The second confusion is the assumption that wealth is simply acquired. In fact it has to be created, a process which often involves breathtaking imagination and ingenuity. For the natural contents of the earth do not come ready to hand labelled as resources. As mere material objects they are useless until someone has the insight to perceive their utility in satisfying human wants. That the hundred-million-year-old remains of molluscs could be transformed into a myriad series of well-controlled explosions turning wheels is almost beyond the bounds of sane belief. Yet we *do* drive petrol-driven cars.

Accordingly, to think that wealth is simply acquired, by grabbing for oneself what is waiting ready-made to be shared out amongst us all, displays gross ignorance. Resources are created and put to useful work by human effort and imagination. There can be no moral objection to rewarding the conspicuously able and energetic with a proportionately larger share of the wealth they have helped to create. And the case is strengthened by the pragmatic consideration that the lack of such an incentive will certainly inhibit some workers and entrepreneurs from wealth-creation and so further depress the living standards of the worst-off. Indeed, changing relative prices, wages and profits perform an indispensable signalling function in a market economy. Of course competitive markets operate only in a framework of law which safeguards life and property and specifies minimum standards.

This assertion will no doubt be contested on the grounds that capitalism already leaves the poor as impoverished as they could be. Thus Morland, apparently referring to totalitarian socialism, remarks that the 'cost is almost *worse* than self-interested individualism' (italics added) and goes on to urge us to become 'actors in the right play, i.e. that of the oppressed'.[9]

Such a view is at variance with the facts of history. Under a broadly free market, when wages were supposedly at subsistence level, the population of England and Wales grew fourfold (1801-1900). Admittedly, working conditions were often harsh and oppressive by later standards but they gradually improved and the factory hands and millions of consumers benefited from the cheap cotton clothes, the soap and so on which were produced. The most successful capitalists were mass-producers, whose products enabled the masses to enjoy a progressively rising standard of living previously available only to a privileged minority. And today the new capitalist oases in Asia are doing much more to abolish poverty than African socialists, who bewail the power of the multinationals. The best form of overseas aid is to set a good capitalist example for those with the wit to follow it.

Only wealth can overcome poverty and nothing creates wealth like 'capitalism'.

Conclusion

The critique of post-materialist tendencies in contemporary Christianity can be summarized in two premises and a conclusion. First, it has been suggested that the material and the spiritual are not irreconcilable opposites competing for our attention but complementary aspects of life. Material objects without an infusion of spirit are devoid of meaning: spiritual endeavour without material means is doomed to failure. Second, it has been argued that involuntary poverty is evil in its frustration of human purposes and offers no more reliable road to God than does material security. The conclusion is twofold. The argument shows that we need to create wealth in order to make spiritual and humanitarian impulses effective and in particular to get rid of poverty. And it is reasonable to believe, on the basis of historical evidence, that capitalism is the best wealth-creating system yet devised.

NOTES

1 *Community, Wealth and Taxation,* The Laity Commission (1982) p. 17.

2 ibid., p. 16.

3 The emergence of post-materialism has attracted the attention of political and social scientists on both sides of the Atlantic. See S. M. Lipset, 'Whatever happened to the proletariat?', *Encounter,* June 1981. He writes that post-materialism seems to have originated in the protest movements of the 1960s, in 'opposition to the Viet Nam War, struggles for Civil Rights, Women's Lib and Gay Liberation, and Environmentalism' (p. 25). Its characteristic concerns are with '*non-economic* or *social* issues — a clean environment; a better culture; equal status for women and minorities; the quality of education; international relations; greater

democratisation; and a more permissive morality' (p. 24). See also G. Dawson, 'Social Science and Anti-Business Culture', *Journal of Further and Higher Education,* Autumn 1981; and 'Unfitting Teachers to Teach: Sociology in the Training of Teachers', in D. C. Anderson, ed., *The Pied Pipers of Education,* The Social Affairs Unit, 1981.

4 The Rev. David Morland OSB, *The Eucharist and Justice,* Infoform for the Catholic Information Office (1980) pp. 24-5. Morland overlooks the fact that stripping away ecclesiastical riches may further impoverish the poor, by depriving them of an adequate focus for the expression of their religious feelings. The general point is that material splendour has a role to play in celebrating the glory of God. Just as a royal wedding can lift the hearts of people whose lives are normally drab, so can the grandeur of a cathedral overwhelm mundane anxieties and evoke the numinous.

5 'The sort of "stripping away" that this involves for the Western Church is . . . a condition of its own salvation' ibid., p. 21.

6 The dehumanizing effects of extreme deprivation on the Ik, an African tribe, are described in C. Turnbull, *The Mountain People,* Simon and Schuster 1972. They steal food from children, the sick and the aged and their behaviour becomes worse when the food supply improves: 'If they had been mean and greedy and selfish before with nothing to be mean and greedy and selfish over, now that they had something they really excelled themselves in what would be an insult to animals to call bestiality' (p. 280).

7 'Midway this way of life we're bound upon,
   I woke to find myself in a dark wood,
   Where the right road was wholly lost and gone.'
       Dante, *The Divine Comedy.*

8 The Laity Commission, op. cit., p. 17.

9 Morland, op. cit., pp. 7 and 20.

2

Unchristian Critiques of Multinationals: The Case of South Africa

Bertie Everard

The background

In the last decade or so there has been a crescendo of criticism from the Church about the activities of multinational companies. A spate of reports, articles and books has appeared, the most recent being a symposium of essays, *Transnational Corporations,* commissioned jointly by the Church of England and the British Council of Churches.[1] Some commentators[2] have traced this onslaught back to the campaign against apartheid in the Republic of South Africa, which was certainly in the spotlight of attention during the 1970s. Nowadays, however, the critics operate on a much broader front.

Let it be said at the outset that many Christians (including this author) believe that it is the right and the duty of the Church corporate and of individual Christians to speak out against both apartheid, which is a fundamental contradiction of the Christian doctrine of man,[3] and against what Edward Heath once called 'the unacceptable face of capitalism'. The moral authority of the Church and the influence that stems therefrom are a necessary counterbalance against unethical behaviour in this imperfect world.

The indictment

This paper is not an apologia for multinationals (two of the essays in *Transnational Corporations* put their case well) or for business in general, still less for the South African government. The issues discussed are the unchristian manner and form that the criticism is apt to take, the unchristian assumptions that frequently underlie it, and the damaging, counterproductive consequences that stem from such criticism. Some of it can appear so bereft of Christian values like truth, integrity and charity towards one's neighbour

21

that it drove one noted industrialist to tell the World Council of Churches Consultation on Transnational Corporations at Geneva in 1977:

> I read the proceedings of your previous meeting at Cartigny with growing anger. My anger arose from the prejudice, ignorance and intellectual dishonesty which are displayed there. I am asked to believe that I and my colleagues . . . are parties to a cheap conspiracy to defraud the poorer nations of the world . . . we are all uniformly accused . . . you have a clear decision to make, which is whether or not you want to join the witch burners.[4]

The methodology of much of the criticism seems to be to impugn the motives of those who direct business affairs, to smear the character and ethics of business organizations in general, to distort the nature of capitalism and the market economy, to ignore, disparage or minimize the positive benefits that multinationals bring to the countries in which they operate, to arraign them in public often on the most slender evidence, and to generate a hostile climate aimed at exhorting the general public to take positive action (e.g. the 'Kit Kat Boycott', or selling shares in companies with South African subsidiaries). The resemblance of some of these church reports to Marxist literature is striking.

Thus the Rev. Canon G. R. Dunstan, lately Professor of Moral and Social Theology at King's College, University of London, observes that:

> the most widely heard Christian prescriptions for South Africa today, those coming from the World Council of Churches and the Roman Catholic 'liberationist' movements, are in reality the dictates of a political ideology . . . clothing themselves in Biblical or Christian language.[5]

The Rev. Canon M. West correctly draws attention[6] to the bewildered resentment of managers who are the butt of such criticism, but fails to point out that it is more its manner that causes hurt than any well-intentioned, well-informed and well-aimed comments on the way they conduct their business. However, it is not the ruffled feathers of industrialists that is the saddest consequence: it is the risk that the misguided churches 'will prove to be the perpetuators of poverty and the architects of underdevelopment'.[7]

Underlying attitudes

At the back of much of the criticism from the Church is the ideological dislike of the so-called 'profit motive' and the hoary anti-business attitudes in our church and academic culture which denigrate those who devote their lives to generating wealth. In a guide to basic Christian ideas entitled 'Christians and Wealth',[8] and edited by Canon West, the following sentences appear:

> Poverty . . . is always an evil because it is the outcome of the wickedness of the rich and powerful.

> In the fifth century St Jerome wrote, 'unless one person has lost, another cannot find'. Therefore I believe the popular proverb is very true — 'the rich person is either an unjust person or the heir of one'.

But surely poverty has more than one cause: it is not uniquely caused by the wicked, powerful, rich bogeymen of our left wing clergy, and surely there exist some just, rich sons and daughters of just parents? Moreover, the quotation from St Jerome is used to imply that there is a constant amount of wealth to go round: if one man acquires wealth, another must suffer poverty in equal measure. This, however, is not the case: the sum total of wealth in the world can and does increase, so that people can increase their wealth by having the same share of a larger cake. Above all, the sterile notion that in economics one man's gain is another's loss ignores the elementary proposition that trade between willing buyer and willing seller benefits both parties. This truism is indeed the foundation of the division of labour on which all economic progress ultimately rests.

The way in which this sort of thinking is applied to the question of British investment in South Africa is illustrated by the following quotation from a recent Church of England report:[9]

> We [Britain] cling tenaciously to this investment because returns are high: returns are high because black wages are low: we are part of the system of exploitation.

The implied guilt is then visited upon employees, as exemplified by a quotation from an unpublished letter written by Rev. Dr J. P. Brown, General Secretary of the Uniting Churches in Australia:

We hope that employees will realise that the company they serve has played a major role in the support of cruelty and racism in South Africa.

Yet it is not necessary to be an economist to understand that while black wages are by our standards 'low', the readiness of black workers to compete to accept them is proof positive that the wages are more attractive than any available alternative source of income.

The corporate Churches' campaign

The World Council of Churches seems to encourage such criticism in what has been described as 'by far the most irresponsible anti-multinational company polemic produced by any international organisation'.[10] It aims to raise the consciousness of churches and individual Christians about the supposedly oppressive role multinationals play in all parts of the world, to assist the channelling of resources to support action against multinationals, to work to dismantle the economic and techno-logical power supposedly concentrated in their hands, and to lobby the UN Commission on Transnational Corporations so as to promote these ends. It generally ignores the positive contribution of multinational activities and condemns activities that have been considered positive as public relations tactics used simply to deceive.

As part of this world movement, the British Council of Churches, in a pamphlet, *South Africa and Ourselves,* prominently reported in *The Guardian,*[11] called on churches to press companies to withdraw from South Africa, boycott products, ask questions at AGMs and to campaign for progressive disinvestment. As a result, companies are unproductively bombarded with questions from local authorities, trade unions, university administrators and members of the general public, often based on gross misapprehensions.

The individual churches, Anglican, Methodist, United Reformed, Society of Friends, Roman Catholic and Church of Scotland have all published statements or resolutions in similar vein. Some, such as an Anglican paper with an impartial-sounding title, *The Churches and the Multinationals — How to Get into the*

Debate, strike the author as unbalanced and partisan in content.[12]

Yet equally committed Christians, economists and sociologists, black and white, who are just as knowledgeable and no less abhor apartheid, hold that disinvestment would be counterproductive. How is it, then, that the Church corporate has been persuaded to adopt so critical and damaging a stance towards companies that trade in South Africa, and to seek to discourage emigration to South Africa, instead of supporting those Christian businessmen who try to colonize the Devil's territory and reform it from within? B. E. P. Smith, a man who spent twenty-five years in business in South Africa before entering the ministry, criticizes the churches who advocate disinvestment and cessation of immigration:

> Such negative, destructive policies will do untold harm and serve not one iota to the peaceful solutions of the problems facing southern Africa. If the churches of the UK desire, as indeed we all do, to see changes in southern African society, then they should actively encourage positive, constructive policies such as an increase in the right type of immigration, an increase in capital investment in this country and its neighbours and the encouragement of more and more contact.[13]

Critique of a critique: a case study

It is instructive to analyse the research reports that purport to justify actions that the churches recommend. Take the case of the Stares report, *ICI in South Africa,*[14] one of several reports from Christian Concern for South Africa, a body set up in 1972 to engage in a dialogue with British companies, their shareholders, and their customers. For many years, ICI's operations in South Africa, through their associated company AECI and their subsidiary ICI (South Africa), have contributed massively to economic development. Sir Harry Oppenheimer, a leading liberal outspoken in his criticism of the South African government,[15] spent many years as Chairman of AECI. The benefits ICI have conferred on the South African people by their presence, in terms of reducing poverty and providing jobs, and by their enlightened employment policies (relative to the norm in that country) far outweigh any damage or suffering that their presence could conceivably be said to cause. The company is typical of many others of whom R. Whyte, formerly of the World Bank, has written:

> . . . the impact of TNCs in Africa and Asia is overwhelmingly positive. They have made an indispensable contribution to raising world living standards and need to be encouraged rather than denigrated.[16]

Yet the Stares report implies on the first page that ICI has 'very considerable power' and is in a 'favourable relationship' with the South African state which has 'allowed it' to have a monopoly. It makes 'a significant contribution to munitions and the uranium industry', the implied accusation being that ICI is helping South Africa to develop nuclear and other weapons for use against the blacks. This is further developed on page 2 so as to leave the reader with the impression that ICI is significantly and clandestinely assisting the South African government in this activity. The phrase 'munitions industry' appears in the same sentence as 'uranium' several times. It is true that ICI manufactures sulphuric acid, some of which is sold on the open market for the extraction of uranium which is predominantly used for power generation, but this hardly amounts to collaboration in the manufacture of nuclear weapons. The truth is that ICI is not involved in the manufacture of munitions (as distinct from industrial explosives), nor has it any direct technical or financial connection with the uranium industry in South Africa.

A further juxtaposition on page 4 of the phrases: 'reported involvement . . . in the production of tear gas for the South African security forces . . . involvement in the uranium industry . . . serious ethical questions . . .' builds up a picture that is more than the sum of its parts, namely that ICI is probably in league with the South African government in preparing for war against oppressed blacks.

On page 5 we read of a 'massive programme of expansion . . . (despite) stark evidence of increasing racial polarisation and mounting violence . . . clear that the group is raising new money . . . to finance a markedly greater stake in the apartheid system'. Some might infer that ICI is recklessly and with malice aforethought investing new money in the strengthening of South

African political oppression. Throughout the report, its author is disdainful of the profit motive, and appears not to be aware of the process of wealth-creation in any economic system. By page 8 he calls for 'the termination of ICI's involvement, through the supply of military material, in the repression by the South African security forces of the black communists in South Africa'.

To lend respectability to the report, an appendix lists the names of thirty-three eminent Christians who are members of the CCSA Council. The vast majority are either ministers of religion or church officers. Only one Christian businessman appears on the list, the former director of the Manchester Business School, who also directs a business. If the Council is going to sponsor documents that comment on business affairs as well as on ethical matters, surely it should take steps to become informed about the world businessmen live in: in this way their Christian witness might be put more in touch with the world of economic realities rather than the idealism of Mr Stares' world.

Other examples

This is not an isolated instance: another such report, endorsed by CCSA, *A Code for Misconduct*,[17] contains similar emotive language and quotes not a single instance of any British company doing anything creditable in South Africa. It purports to show that the EEC Code of Conduct for firms operating in South Africa has been ineffective.

Reports such as these, whether coming from the Church or the UN Commission on Transnational Corporations, might be taken as impartial, apolitical, well researched and beyond reproach. They are certainly quoted as such by trade unions searching for ammunition with which to castigate companies and generally to erode the trust that employees repose in their management. Is it any wonder some South Africans are cautious in their approach to trade unionism when they see the effects in the UK of politicization of the movement along Marxist ideological lines?

The assumptions underlying another CCSA report, *Black Trade Unions in South Africa: The Responsibilities of British Companies*,[18] are patently left-wing and antagonistic towards business. Even what the author calls 'The Personnel Management Approach' is besmirched, and the works council mechanisms on which for

27

years some of the more enlightened British firms have successfully built up their industrial relations are belittled as 'high principled rhetoric'. What observers less imbued with Marxist ideology would see as progressive, is dismissed in these words:

> While many companies may therefore like to picture personnel management as a humane and enlightened bridge between a past based on coercion and a future based on negotiated consent, there are strong reasons for believing that it is a largely unworkable blind alley which could also frustrate subsequent attempts to construct a more sustainable and less paternalistic system of industrial relations.

One wonders what the Institute of Personnel Management would make of that!

The need for balance

What is clearly needed in this arena is more balance and rigour of thought, deeper and less prejudiced understanding of the nature of business and business decisions, and more competent analysis of what brings about desirable change. The Rev. Canon Dunstan is one commentator who clearly recognizes that the moral question is inseparable from the practical question and from estimates of probable consequences of such action as disinvestment. In the paper referred to previously (see note 5) he says that he cannot go along with 'fashionable ecclesiastical moralism, to withdraw investment from companies operating in South Africa, and so keep your hands clean. This is simply to purchase an easy conscience (not a clear one) at the expense of sacrificing responsibility . . .'

He is supported by Ivor Richard QC (former Labour MP and now EEC Commissioner for Social Affairs) who, in commenting on our trade relations with South Africa, said 'Gesture politics doesn't work. It is transparent, intellectually dishonest and morally specious.'[19] And, as Barber and Spicer point out in a useful analysis of the problem,[20] 'for every argument that favours sanctions, another can be found to counter it'.

It now seems at last to be dawning on the Church that questions related to multinationals and to South Africa are of immense complexity, such that it is perfectly possible for equally committed and informed Christians to hold divergent points of view, thus rendering the stance of the more partisan church spokesmen even less appropriate. As the then Bishop of Truro said in the General Synod debate on 8 November 1979, 'The greater our objections to apartheid' (he could have said, multinationals), 'the greater the temptation to espouse the more extreme positions.' And temptation it is: a temptation happily resisted in the Church's latest pronouncement on *Transnational Corporations*[21] with the balance of which few Christian businessmen or economists, recognizing the humility of the editors' approach, could reasonably complain.

However, the damage that has been done by ideological mudslinging cannot so easily be undone, and in the process the Church has lost respect. It deserves better of its more professional spokesmen and advisers, for the cause they espouse is of the deepest concern to all Christians, whether in business or pulpit. In the spirit of Christ's exhortation, 'First cast out the beam out of thine own eye: and then thou shalt see clearly to cast out the mote out of thy brother's eye'.[22] At the risk of being told 'Physician, heal thyself', I dare to suggest the need for a critics' code of practice. Clauses in such a code might be:

1 Thou shalt not bear false witness against thy neighbour's business, however worthy thy cause.
2 Thou shalt verify thy sources of information and not believe everything thou readest.
3 Thou shalt not dishonestly use innuendo, rhetoric and emotional language to frighten readers into thy camp.
4 Thou shalt not worship graven images of Marxism but shalt base the manner and content of thy criticism on Judaeo-Christian theology.
5 Thou shalt not falsely attribute base motives to directors and managers to explain all that thou revilest in the market economy, lest most prove just stewards seeking after good, or at least the lesser evil.[23]
6 Thou shalt not covet thy neighbour's profits even to give to the poor, especially if he puts them to good use.
7 Thou shalt not complain of the repatriation of profits, for it is written, 'Invest your money in foreign trade and one of these days you will make a profit.'[24]

NOTES

1 P. Brett and A. Dyson, ed., *Transnational Corporations: Confronting the Issues,* CIO Publishing 1983.

2 J. Schwarzbach, *The World Council of Churches,* a report by Organisation Resources Counselors Inc., New York.

3 'So there is no difference between Jews and Gentiles, between slaves and free men: you are all one in union with Christ Jesus' Galatians 3.28; cf. Colossians 3.11 (Good News Bible).

4 G. Chandler, *Self Understanding of TNCs,* Speech at Geneva Consultation of World Council of Churches, 13-18 June 1977.

5 G. R. Dunstan, *South Africa: Sanctions and Disinvestment: An Examination of the Economic Effects and Ethical Issues,* Christian Association of Business Executives, 1979.

6 Brett and Dyson, op. cit.

7 G. Chandler, op. cit.

8 *Work in Life,* Council of Industrial Mission in Hertfordshire and Bedfordshire (Winter 1980) no. 3, p. 3.

9 *Facing the Facts: the UK and South Africa,* Church of England, 1982.

10 Schwarzbach, op. cit.

11 *South Africa and Ourselves,* BCC and CCSA, November 1982, reported in *The Guardian,* 23 November 1982.

12 *The Churches and the Multinationals – How to Get into the Debate,* Working Paper no. 5, Church of England Synod Board for Social Responsibility Industrial Committee, December 1978.

13 B. E. P. Smith, *Reform,* URC, June 1978, p. 29.

14 R. Stares, *ICI in South Africa,* Christian Concern for South Africa, March 1977.

15 See, for example, H. F. Oppenheimer, 'Why Apartheid Must End', *Daily Express,* 29 June 1978.

16 Brett and Dyson, op. cit.

17 B. Rogers, *A Code for Misconduct,* CCSA, 1980.

18 R. Stares, *Black Trade Unions in South Africa: The Responsibilities of British Companies,* CCSA, October 1977.

19 *British Trade with South Africa: A question of National Interest,* UK South Africa Trade Association, 1978.

20 J. Barber and M. Spicer, 'Sanctions against South Africa — Options for the West', *International Affairs* (July 1979) vol. 55.

21 Brett and Dyson, op. cit.

22 Matthew 7.5 (King James' Version).

23 K. B. Everard, The Christian Layman in Management, *Industrial and Commercial Training* (April 1980) vol. 12, p. 140.

24 Ecclesiastes 11.1 (Good News Bible).

3

Ecclesiastical Economics of the Third World: Envy Legitimized

Peter Bauer*

> I shall speak of the foul sin of envy,
> which is grief at another's prosperity.
>
> Chaucer, *The Parson's Tale*

Since Vatican II, authoritative Roman Catholic documents have increasingly included or endorsed several myths about poverty, particularly poverty in the Third World. The myths are encouraged by such figures as Dom Helder Camara and Monsenor Lopez Trujillo, Secretary-General of the Latin-American Bishops' Conference, and they seem to be endorsed in Encyclical and Pontifical letters of Pope Paul VI, *Populorum Progressio* (1967) and *Octogesima Adveniens* (1971).[1] Such documents reflect an increasing consensus.

The four central myths are:

Myth I

That differences in income are 'inequalities' which are the results of injustice. The poor are poor because the rich have made them so while enriching themselves. At a national level, poor countries are poor *because* rich countries are rich.

According to Monsenor Alfonso Lopez Trujillo: 'The United States and Canada are rich because the peoples of Latin America are poor. They have built their wealth on top of us.'[2] And according to Helder Camara: 'It [rural poverty] is not a local problem: it is a national problem, even a continental problem. You know that the prices of our raw materials have always been set in the great decision-making centres of the world . . . And

* This chapter is a condensation by Dr D. Anderson of a chapter appearing in P. T. (now Lord) Bauer, *Reality and Rhetoric: Studies in the Economics of Development* (Weidenfeld & Nicolson and Harvard University Press, 1984).

while we [the Catholic Church] supported what amounted to social disorder, the United Nations were proclaiming that two-thirds of mankind live in inhuman conditions of misery and hunger.'[3]

Subsidiary themes support the main theme that inequality means injustice. A major problem is the question of 'the fairness in the exchange of goods and in the division of wealth between individuals and countries' (*Octogesima Adveniens OA7*). The economic system left to itself widens international economic differences: '. . . rich peoples enjoy rapid growth whereas the poor develop slowly. The imbalance is on the increase: some produce a surplus of foodstuffs, others cruelly black them and see their exports made uncertain' (*Populorum Progressio PP8*).

Again, 'in trade between developed and under-developed economies, conditions are too disparate and the degrees of genuine freedom available too unequal' (*PP61*). This inequality is responsible for the persistent deterioration in the terms of trade of primary producers. 'The value of manufactured goods is rapidly increasing and they can always find an adequate market. On the other hand, raw materials produced by under-developed countries are subject to wide and sudden fluctuations in price, a state of affairs far removed from the progressively increasing value of industrial products. . . . The poor nations remain ever poor while the rich ones become still richer' (*PP57*).

Myth II

Myth two is that governments always act for the common good. Under the heading 'Programmes and Planning' Pope Paul VI writes: 'It pertains to the public authorities to choose, even to lay down, the objectives to be pursued, in economic development the ends to be achieved, and the means of attaining them, and it is for them to stimulate all the forces engaged in this common activity' (*PP33*). These tasks must be left to governments, to the representatives of political power 'which is the natural and necessary link for ensuring the cohesion of the social body . . . *It always intervenes with careful justice and with devotion to the common good* for which it holds final responsibility' (*OA46* italics added).

Myth III

Because income differences are inequalities, unjust inequalities, and because governments act for the common good, politically organized income redistribution is desirable. Individual action is insufficient to deal with the problems. Collective action is required, and to be effective has to be political. This is so partly because of the magnitude of the problems. But the more important reason why action has to be collective and political is that, in the explicit opinion of the Pope, governments always act for the common good (*OA*, p. 46, quoted above). The efforts should take the form primarily of concerted international actions and plans.

The proposals revolve around the theme of politically organized redistribution. The primary theme is the urgent need for official international wealth transfers to redress existing international inequality and injustice and thereby to promote development and peace. (The prescription is predictable, because whenever a speaker or writer describes income differences as 'inequalities', he is likely to advocate redistribution).

These official transfers are necessary 'to further the progress of poorer peoples, to encourage social justice among nations, to offer to less developed nations the means whereby they can further their own progress' (*PP5*). For this purpose 'all available resources should be pooled' (*PP43*).

Myth IV

Land redistribution is crucial. One group which is singled out for condemnation are landowners whose 'landed estates impede the general prosperity because they are extensive, unused or poorly used, or because they bring hardship to peoples or are detrimental to the interests of the country so that the common good sometimes demands their expropriation' (*PP24*).

These are myths.

The facts and Myth I

Poverty is not caused by the rich. Paul VI does not examine the reasons behind income differences or behind the conditions of the poor, except for the assertion that poverty is the result of misconduct by the rich, which is generally misleading and often the exact opposite of the truth. Income differences, including riches and poverty, cannot be discussed sensibly without looking at their background. Individuals, groups and societies can be poor for any number of different reasons. Thus a person may become poor because he has habitually overspent a large income. But he may be poor for circumstances entirely beyond his control such as incurable disease, confiscation of his assets, or the restriction of his opportunities. Both individuals and groups may be materially unambitious. Contrast for instance the conduct and position of Malays and Chinese in Malaysia. Again, if many poor people survive longer in a less developed country, this depresses per capita incomes and leads to what is habitually termed a worsening income distribution both within the particular country and relatively to richer countries. Conversely, if more of the poor die or a society reverts to subsistence production, this brings about more equal incomes within a country, accompanied by a rise in per capita incomes in the former case and a decline in the latter case.

Group differences in economic performance abound in the Third World. For instance, in Malaysia the Chinese economic performance has been far superior to that of Malays, in spite of long-standing discrimination against them. Indeed, their success in recent years has been the cornerstone of official economic policy. (Other examples of the relative success of groups discriminated against are commonplace in economic history.) These considerations make clear that equality of opportunity, in the sense of an open society, does not bring about substantial equality of incomes, but on the contrary results in wide income differences.

In Latin America the prosperity of the landowners, industrialists and merchants has not been achieved at the expense of the poor. The economic conditions of the poorest groups, the Indians of Central and Southern America and the Negro slaves in Brazil, are no worse, and in many ways far better, than were those of their ancestors. The economic conditions of Negroes in Brazil do not differ greatly from those of Africans in the more advanced parts of Black Africa.

The notion that the incomes of the more prosperous have somehow been achieved at the expense of the less prosperous has had a long and disastrous history. In its consequences it is perhaps the most pernicious of all economic misconceptions. The persecution of economically productive but politically unpopular and ineffective minorities in the Third World is perhaps the primary example today.

In fact there are other neglected causes of poverty. Bishop Bududira[4] has argued that the local cultures in Africa and elsewhere in the Third World obstruct material progress. The Bishop insists that economic improvement of a person depends on the person himself, notably on his mental attitudes, especially on his attitude to work. Unquestioning acceptance of nature and of its vagaries is widespread in Africa and elsewhere in the Third World. Man sees himself not as making history, but as suffering it.

To regard life as inexorably ordained by fate prevents a person from developing his or her potential. The obligations of the extended family system stifle ambition and creative imagination. Initiative is inhibited further by dependence on tribal groups. These groups suppress innovation and regard efforts for change and improvements as forms of rebellion. The Bishop concludes that the message of Christ frees people from the shackles of tribal thinking. It leads to greater sense of personal responsibility. The required changes can best be achieved by Christian groups working with local communities.

Some of these ideas used to be familiar. They are very rarely heard nowadays. The translator's comment on the article was that only an African could now write such an article. In that sense the ideas are novel. *Ex Africa semper aliquid novi.*

The facts and Myths II & III

There are, of course, major exceptions to the general proposition that the incomes of the prosperous are earned. Predominantly these exceptions are incomes derived from government-conferred privileges. Such privileges are especially significant and widespread in the extremely politicized societies of the Third World. Their many forms include state subsidies, restrictions on competition, allocations of licences and favoured forms of employment. These incomes are not what the Pope and other clerics have in mind in their attacks on 'inequality'. Such incomes do not feature in discussions of international differences in income. And in the national sphere it is the papal view that governments act for the general good, so that the results of their policies cannot be the subject for redress through politically organized redistribution. Finally, egalitarian discourse is addressed to income differences as such, not to privileged incomes *vis-à-vis* other incomes.

The case for income redistribution becomes yet more dubious when it is remembered that politically organized redistribution is apt to aggravate the lot of the poorest (as well as to aggrandize those who organize the transfers). To begin with, state organized redistribution often benefits middle income groups at the expense both of the rich and of the poor. This is now widely recognized in redistribution within a country, especially when the benefits accruing to the administrators of these policies are also taken into account. Moreover, redistribution inhibits enterprise and effort as well as the accumulation and productive deployment of capital, retarding the rise in living standards, including those of the poorest.

The adverse effects of redistribution on the living standards of the poorest are perforce ignored when income and wealth are envisaged, as they often are, as being extracted from other people, or somehow achieved at their expense by depriving them of what they had or could have had. They are regarded as fixed totals rather than as the results of productive activities and processes over time. However, in market economies at any rate incomes are normally earned; they are not shares in a pre-existing total.

In egalitarian discourse the notion that the well-off have prospered at the expense of the poor is rarely far below the surface. This notion is useful or even necessary for the moral plausibility of politically organized redistribution. Without such an underpinning the case for redistributive taxation (which in effect is partial confiscation), or for other forms of expropriation, is not self-evident. Why should social justice mean substantially equal incomes? Why is it obviously unjust that those who contribute more to production should have higher incomes than those who contribute less?

The facts and Myth IV

Land is not the issue. Lack of natural resources, including land, has little or nothing to do with the poverty of individuals or of societies. Amidst abundant land and natural resources the Indians before Columbus remained wretchedly poor, without domestic animals and without even the wheel, when much of Europe with far less land was already rich. In the less developed world today many millions of extremely poor people have abundant cultivatable land. Over much of Asia, Africa and Latin America very large numbers of extremely poor and backward people live in areas where cultivatable but uncultivated land is free or extremely cheap. The small size and low productivity of farms and the presence of landless workers in such areas reflect not the shortage of land but primarily the lack of ambition, enterprise and skill.

Of course, land which has been improved by the efforts and savings of productive people is the target for demands for redistribution even where unimproved land is plentiful. Who would not welcome a free gift of valuable assets? Land on its own is unproductive, and yields nothing of value to mankind. It becomes productive as a result of ambition, perceptiveness, resourcefulness and effort — attitudes and characteristics very unequally present among different individuals, groups and societies.

Sustained prosperity, as distinct from occasional windfalls, owes little or nothing to natural resources: witness West Germany, Switzerland, Japan, Singapore, Hong Kong and Taiwan, among many other instances. The wide differences in economic performance between individuals and groups in the same country with access to the same natural resources throws into relief the personal and cultural differences behind economic achievement.

The conditions of the poorest and most backward people throughout the Third World, such as tribal societies, pygmies and aborigines, have nothing to do with lack of land, Western exploitation or the activities of ethnic minorities. These groups have few contacts either with the West or with economically active ethnic minorities. They also have abundant land at their disposal. Much the same applies to the causes of famine and to the lack of so-called basic facilities. For instance, the famines in sparsely populated African countries such as Ethiopia, the Sahel, Tanzania, Uganda and Zaire reflect the low level of subsistence or near subsistence activity, perpetuated or aggravated by the lack of public security and by damaging policies such as official suppression of trading activity, forced collectivization and the persecution of productive groups, notably ethnic or tribal minorities. In a few instances continued maintenance of communal (tribal) forms of land tenure also obstructs advance from subsistence production.

Conclusion

These are the four myths. They have three things in common apart from their mythical quality. They would not have been perpetrated if the Church had worked harder at a balanced study of Third World poverty. They will do little to help those who suffer poverty. And they assuredly legitimize envy.

NOTES

1 *Populorum Progressio* 1967 and *Octogesima Adveniens* 1971 are referred to as *PP* and *OA* often with a number indicating the paragraph as numbered in the source. Some passages quoted incorporate and endorse statements from other prominent Catholic sources.

2 Quoted by Malcolm Deas, 'Catholics and Marxists', *London Review of Books*, 19 March 1981.

3 Dom Helder Camara in an interview, 'The Church that Refuses to Think for the Poor', with the London-based magazine *South*, December 1980.

4 Monseigneur Bernard Bududira, Bishop of Bururi in Burundi, part of an article in a French language African journal reproduced in German translation in the Swiss newspaper *Neue Zürcher Zeitung*, 4-5 January 1981.

Black Crime, the 'Racist' Police and Fashionable Compassion

P. A. J. Waddington

From reservations about figures to attributions of racism

It appears sometimes to be assumed by 'progressive' Christians that a compassionate attitude towards issues of 'law and order' is necessarily equated with suspicion of and, indeed, hostility towards the police. Nowhere is this assumption more apparent than in discussions of police-race relations. It appears to have strongly influenced the author of a Paper, published in 1982 by the Board for Social Responsibility of the Church of England, entitled 'Race and Crime Statistics'.[1] This Paper sought to analyse Metropolitan Police statistics, issued earlier that year,[2] which had, amongst other things, given figures for 'robbery and other violent theft', classified according to the 'victims' perception of the colour of the assailant'. The BSR Paper rekindled the controversy provoked by the publication of these statistics, through its accusation that the police statistics were 'incomplete and poorly presented'[3] — a conclusion widely reported in the press and mass media.[4]

The burden of the Paper's argument was that since there were no figures available regarding the proportions of people of different ethnic origin in each of the 24 Metropolitan Police districts, it was impossible to say whether the preponderance of black suspects in some areas was 'disproportionate' or not. Thus, the fact that in Lambeth nearly 2000 victims identified their assailants as 'coloured' compared with 327 who identified them as 'white'[5] might simply reflect the proportion of non-white to white residents in those areas. In addition, the Paper repeated accusations, made earlier in the press,[6] that these figures had been released for racialist motives. Indeed, in its general discussion of crime statistics, which was the preamble to the analysis of the Metropolitan Police statistics, there was the strong implication that the police are generally racialist and that patterns of arrest reflect this racialism.[7]

Possessing the additional moral authority of a Church of England publication, this paper promoted the view that the police are racialist and that the problems of race and crime in the inner cities is a myth. Certainly, this is how the Paper was treated by the press and mass media. It undoubtedly made a significant contribution to the decision of the Metropolitan Police not to issue comparable figures a year later.

Two issues

It is necessary to separate two issues. The first, is whether the police figures showed blacks to be disproportionately involved in street crimes. In this connection the BSR Paper is correct, the necessary information is lacking. However, it is important to note that it was the press, not the police, who drew this inference. The Paper provides no evidence that the police did other than issue valid statistics cautiously and correctly labelled 'victims' perceptions of the colour of their assailant'. The second issue is whether the police are racialist and the problem of crime in the inner cities is a myth. Neither of these suppositions is sustained by the Paper. The clear implication that the Metropolitan Police issued 'incomplete and poorly presented' statistics and orchestrated a press coverage that was 'at times misleading and often erroneous'[8] for racialist motives, rests upon no solid foundation.

It is this second accusation, that the police are racialist, that appears to reflect the underlying assumption held by 'progressive' Christians, that a compassionate attitude necessarily requires antipathy to the police. Such an assumption blinds those who hold it to the distinction between the two issues described above. It assumes that if the press misinterpreted the statistics, the police must thereby be tainted with racialism and the figures can have no significance. It is, in short, a prejudice.

Like many prejudices, this anti-police prejudice rests on a grain of truth which is exaggerated and distorted. For example, misleading impressions *can* be created by statistics such as those issued by the Metropolitan Police. Criminal statistics are notoriously difficult to interpret correctly. The fundamental problem is that because not all crimes that are committed are reported to the police, these statistics do not reflect accurately the extent and pattern of crime. As the recent British Crime Survey shows,[9] only about a quarter to a third of even the most serious offences are reported to the police. Reliance on official figures of 'crimes known to the police' may, therefore, be misleading because of the influence of extraneous factors influencing rates at which offences are reported. For example, the British Crime Survey found that the *only* category of crime to be reported 100 per cent of the time was that of thefts of motor cars;[10] presumably a reflection of insurance requirements. Just as we obtain a distorted picture of crime, with serious crimes under-reported and 'auto-crime' fully reported, so too we might get a distorted picture of changes in patterns of crime. The National Household Survey has been collecting information regarding burglary for the past ten years, which indicates that the actual increase in that crime has been nearer 10 per cent, rather than the 30 per cent shown in official statistics.[11]

Applied to the issue of race and crime, this argument concludes that it is unsafe to rely on such statistics in making any assessment of black involvement in 'street crime'. They may be simply an outcome of reporting tendencies and procedures.

Exaggeration, distortion, and anti-police prejudice

The grain of truth in this argument should alert us to bear in mind the purpose for which official statistics are collected and to appreciate the dangers of using statistics collected for one purpose for quite another. However, the exaggeration and distortion entailed in the argument is the suggestion that criminal statistics have little or no utility. Certainly, these statistics are not collected for the purpose of simply describing social conditions, as might a social survey. People report crimes and the police record them for very practical reasons. People want the police to 'do something' and the police need to know what they are expected to 'do something' about. The fact that people may not want the police to 'do something' about some crimes of which they are the victim (the under-reporting problem) does *not* mean that the crimes which *are* reported have no significance. The British Crime Survey found that by far the most common reason for not reporting offences was because victims perceived them as too trivial to warrant it.[12] The allegation that people may not report offences because of fear or dislike of the police received little support: in the words of the Survey, it was 'rarely mentioned'. In other words, when people report crimes to the police, they are usually saying that they find their victimization intolerable and demand that the police do something about it.

The figures released by the Metropolitan Police can be seen in this light. They show that those offences which annoy, concern, outrage or in some other way prompt members of the public to complain to them, occur more commonly in certain districts, appear to be committed more often in those districts by people described as 'coloured', and have been rapidly increasing. This is the situation as it is presented to the police and to which they have felt obliged to respond.

The decision to publish these figures is directly connected to their practical origins and is quite transparent. As Ronald Butt noted in *The Times*[13] at the time, the police had widely been accused of 'racial harassment', for example, in Brixton prior to the riots of 1981. Their aim in making these figures publicly available was clearly to try to rebut such charges. They were pointing out that in Lambeth, out of a total of 2,493 robberies and violent thefts, victims identified their assailants as 'coloured' on 1,988 occasions, compared with 327 occasions where they were identified as 'white', 72 'mixed gang' and 106 'not known'.[14] Confronted with this situation, the police were bound to conclude that this category of offence in this area was most commonly committed by non-whites and if they were to 'do something' about it, it would be to non-whites that they would need chiefly to direct their attention.

Police reasoning may not have been entirely valid, of course. The reason non-whites were so commonly alleged to have committed such offences may have been because non-whites predominate in the area. There may have been bias in the reporting of these offences. However, as a senior policeman remarked at the time of the Scarman Inquiry, if someone committing an offence is described as 'black' the police do not look for a suspect who is white. Whether stop and search operations such as the ill-starred 'Swamp '81' (widely credited with sparking the Brixton riots) are a sensible or effective response to a situation, no imputation of racialism is required or justified to explain the police response. The public were complaining, on an unprecedented scale, about serious street crimes allegedly committed predominantly by young blacks. The police felt obliged to respond.

Inconsistent analysis and lack of proportion

Was that response, however, as justified as the police statistics might lead us to suppose? A second plank in the BSR Paper's criticism is that the police statistics over-dramatized and distorted the extent of the problem. First, the Paper points out that 'robberies and other violent theft' comprised 'only 3 per cent' of total crimes committed in London.[15] Second, this category of offence included not only so-called 'muggings', but other kinds of offences such as robberies from businesses.[16] Third, that the rate of increase in these offences had been lower for the stereotyped victim of 'muggings', the elderly, than for other groups.[17]

Again, there is a grain of truth in this argument. It *is* easy to get such matters out of proportion. But this BSR argument itself lacks proportion, in seeking to minimize the problem by equating frequency of occurrence with social and moral significance.

To illustrate this minimization, it is instructive to consider another topical issue of race and crime, but one which 'progressives' (rightly) believe to be accorded insufficient attention by the authorities. This is the issue of racially-motivated crimes, which was the subject of a Home Office report in 1981.[18] This report showed that black people were 36 times and Asians 50 times more likely to be the victims of racially-motivated crimes, than were whites. This finding received considerable, albeit short-lived, attention in the press and mass media, and prompted the Select Committee on Home Affairs to inquire further into the problem. The incidence of such racially-motivated crimes is also often cited, as it was in the BSR Paper, to present a more balanced picture of race and crime.

What if we now apply the criticisms levelled at the Metropolitan Police statistics on violent street crimes to the report on racial attacks? First, we would be obliged to note that such attacks comprise 'only' one quarter of 1 per cent of total crimes.[19] In short, it is a much smaller problem, statistically, than is violent street crime. This, of course, does *not* mean that it is an insignificant crime. It is right that we should be concerned about such crimes and a scandal that more concern is not forthcoming from the authorities. However, it also shows that the social and moral significance of crimes is not reducible to the frequency of their occurrence. Violent street crimes may be relatively infrequent, but it is right that the police should be concerned about them.

Second, if the category 'robbery and other violent theft' includes offences other than those normally associated with the term 'mugging', so too does the term 'racial attacks'. This term conjures up the image of physical assault, but, in fact, the report included any 'racially-motivated incident'[20] which encompassed, for example, such damage to property as the daubing of racialist slogans. To say, for example, that the category 'robbery and other violent theft' includes robberies against businesses is at least disingenuous. Apart from the fact that the 'businesses' concerned may include the corner grocery store, since 'robbery' entails the threat or use of physical force, it means that proprietors or employees were the direct victims of violence. Comparatively, therefore, the category 'robbery and other violent theft' is a much closer approximation to our commonsense notions of 'mugging' and the like, than 'racial attacks' is to our notion of physical assault.

The report on racial attacks could not include data on whether and how much these crimes had increased. However, had they revealed the level of increase shown by the police statistics on violent street crime, it is difficult to imagine that they would have been met with other than alarm. The increase in the latter *was* considerable: 34 per cent increase in violent theft; 48 per cent increase in robbery; 40 per cent increase in robbery against the person; and a 27 per cent increase in offences of violence against the elderly.[21] It would surely have been reprehensible if the police had failed to express concern at these figures. Yet, though purporting to keep the problem of violent street crime in proportion, 'progressive' critics such as the BSR have succeeded in achieving an equal but opposite loss of proportion. They minimize the seriousness of such crimes as a social problem.

A black crime problem?

There is not a 'black crime problem' as such, but it is undoubtedly true that violent street crime is a serious problem in certain districts of London and is commonly committed by those described as 'coloured'. This does *not* mean that non-white ethnic minorities are more criminally-inclined than other groups. The BSR Paper is correct in pointing out that involvement in such crimes is largely attributable to living in areas of socio-economic decay and deprivation. It is now simply a fact that non-white ethnic minorities tend to be concentrated in those conditions which have long been associated with crime.

Once again, however, this grain of truth does not support the weight of implications placed upon it. Young blacks may commit more violent street crime because of socio-economic deprivation, but it still remains the duty of the police to arrest and prosecute them. The police are obliged to treat the situation as they find it. Young blacks in the inner-cities come to the attention of the police not because they are *black* but because they are socially deprived: a section of society that have always had more conflictive contact with the police. Those who criticize the police cannot have it both ways; if the relationship between race and crime is spurious — the result of a common association with socio-economic deprivation — then so too is the allegation of racial harassment on the part of the police. Their attention is drawn to the deprived not the black.

Indeed, the pattern of arrests is inconsistent with any simple accusation of racialism, for it is the Irish who are most significantly over-represented in the criminal statistics and Asians who are significantly under-represented. If the pattern of arrests was motivated by racial prejudice amongst the police, it is difficult to imagine why they would pick on the Irish and leave the Asians so conspicuously alone. Indeed, what systematic evidence there is, suggests that the police do not initiate action leading to arrests of anyone, let alone young blacks. Allegations by some, that the police have concentrated on young blacks as part of their campaign against muggers, have not been supported by direct observational evidence of such an 'anti-mugging' squad.

Racism — a facile attribution

Indeed, it is facile to attribute the association of race and crime to racial prejudice on the part of individual police officers. At the time of the Scarman Inquiry and since, there have been repeated allegations that the Metropolitan and other police forces are permeated by racialism.[22] However, despite attempts to prove otherwise, there is no reliable evidence that the police selectively recruit those with racialist attitudes or associated personality dispositions such as authoritarianism and the like.[23] What is evident, however, is that police officers rapidly develop hostile attitudes towards certain ethnic minorities, especially young West Indians.[24] Again, it is facile to attribute this to some process of indoctrination into the informal police sub-culture, the so-called 'canteen culture'.[25]

John Lambert, whose study of police-race relations in Birmingham during the late 1960s was published by the Institute of Race Relations, gives a much more subtle and convincing explanation for police hostility.[26] He was interested in the paradox that although the Irish were over-represented and (at that time) blacks and Asians were under-represented in the criminal statistics, police officers showed no hostility to the Irish but were hostile to blacks and Asians. He observed that increasingly police officers no longer lived in the areas that they policed, but commuted in from the suburbs. It was also the case, and regrettably still is, that few blacks and Asians were members of the police force. Therefore, whilst officers had the opportunity to know Irish people as neighbours and colleagues, their contact with the ethnic minorities was limited to that which occurred during the course of their work.

Whilst blacks and Asians were under-represented in the criminal statistics, the areas of urban decay and social deprivation in which they lived, tended to have higher than average rates of crime. Police officers, erroneously but not unreasonably, associated areas of immigrant concentration with crime. This distorted association of race and crime was further exacerbated by the type of relationship that officers had with the immigrant community during the course of their work. Again, because of the decay and disorganization of the areas in which immigrants lived, the police were frequently called upon to intervene in domestic quarrels, landlord and tenant disputes, and the like. These difficult and delicate so-called 'peace-keeping' duties are disliked by the police because they lack the clarity of law enforcement and threaten to involve them in complex and confused personal relationships and conflicts. Consequently, the police develop a selective perception of immigrants and one which implicitly emphasizes the troublesome nature of such groups. The police rarely have the opportunity, as they do with the Irish, to see that not all immigrants are as they experience them during their work. What has surprised observers, is that this hostility is not translated into discriminatory treatment.

Increasingly, this hostility has been reciprocated especially by young West Indians.[27] Just as the police have selective contact with immigrants, young blacks have selective contact with the police. For the reasons noted above, that contact is usually of the 'peace-keeping' variety. Interventions by the police into personal disputes require the police to act decisively and authoritatively in order to secure what the ordinary citizen cannot, that is, the compliance which enables them to impose a provisional solution and so restore order.[28] From the perspective of young blacks, this is just one more particularly irksome example of white discrimination. As this sense of deprivation and discrimination has been given ideological coherence through Rastafarianism, which regards white society as 'Babylon' and completely evil, so young West Indians have more overtly rejected all manifestations of white authority. This refusal to accept the legitimacy of police authority in their 'peace-keeping' role exacerbates the already difficult relationship between them and the police. Denied the authority to impose a provisional solution, the police must resort to coercion. In so doing they unwittingly confirm the image that young blacks already have of them as the oppressive agents of 'Babylon'. And so the cycle continues into further hostility and mutual suspicion.[29]

Hostility to the police —
a diversion from real problems

No one pretends that the police are perfect or that their role and the way they perform it is above criticism. They cannot solve the problems of the inner cities, but they are required to cope with their more difficult day-to-day manifestations. To blame the police alone for poor police-race relations and to treat their actions with suspicion, is to distract attention from those fundamental problems of urban decay, deprivation and discrimination. It is to indulge in the facile belief that if only police officers can be made, somehow, better men and women, then all will be well.[30] This is not compassion, it is delusion. After all the police reforms are implemented, the conditions in the inner cities with which they must routinely cope, will still remain unchanged.

It should be noted, as the BSR paper itself reminds us, that most crime is intra-racial, not inter-racial. Those who, therefore, suffer most from the high crime rates in our decaying inner cities are those who already suffer significant social deprivation. The lawlessness and disorder to which they are more exposed than most and of which they complain to the police, is yet one further source of social deprivation. Similarly, the insecurity they feel and the threat of becoming a victim of crime is a considerable limitation on their civil liberties. For such people the presence of an effective and responsive police service improves the quality of life and helps to guarantee civil rights.

As Terence Morris wrote, in his sadly prophetic preface to Lambert's study of Birmingham, in August 1968, whilst rejecting those who reject them is a natural response of young blacks,

> The reapers in the field will not be the local councillors, the writers of letters to the local newspapers, the authors of racialist broadsheets, but the agents of order out there on the streets. It will not be of their sowing, but it will be the police who will bare the brunt of what may come.[31]

The BSR Paper illustrates the apparent tendency in much 'progressive' Christian thinking, in that it pays no heed to these difficult complexities. It is far easier and, perhaps, more satisfying to look for scapegoats. However, dispassionate sociological investigation of police-race relations does not support this simplistic approach. It is also necessary that as Christians we recognize these complexities and not reserve compassionate understanding for only one of the parties.

NOTES

1 S. Smith, *Race and Crime Statistics,* Race Relations Fieldwork Background Paper no. 4, Board for Social Responsibility, Church of England, 1982.

2 See *The Times,* 11 March 1982.

3 Smith, op. cit., p. 3.

4 See *The Guardian*, 5 August 1982; *The Times*, 5 August 1982.

5 *The Times,* loc. cit.

6 *The Times,* 12 March 1982.

7 Smith, op. cit., p. 8.

8 ibid., p. 3.

9 M. Hough and P. Mayhew, *British Crime Survey,* H.O.R.S. no. 7, Home Office Research and Planning Unit Report (HMSO 1983) pp. 8-10.

10 ibid., pp. 9-11.

11 ibid., p. 14.

12 ibid., p. 11.

13 *The Times,* 18 March 1982.

14 *The Times,* 11 March 1982.

15 Smith, op. cit., p. 13.

16 ibid.

17 ibid., p. 14.

18 Home Office, *Racial Attacks: Report of a Home Office Study,* November 1981.

19 ibid., p. 10.

20 ibid., pp. 6-8.

21 Smith, op. cit., pp. 13-14.

22 See, for example, P. Scraton, 'Policing and Institutionalized Racism on Merseyside', in D. Cowell, T. Jones, and J. Young, ed., *Policing the Riots* (Junction Books 1982); also, A. Colman and P. Gorman, 'Conservativism, Dogmatism and Authoritarianism in British Police Officers', *Sociology* (1982) vol. 16, pp. 1-11.

23 P. A. J. Waddington, '"Conservativism, Dogmatism and Authoritarianism in British Police Officers": a Comment', *Sociology* (1982) vol. 16, pp. 592-4; P. A. J. Waddington, *Are the Police Fair?,* Social Affairs Unit, 1983.

24 Colman and Gorman, op. cit.

25 J. Brown, *Policing By Multi-Racial Consent.* Bedford Square Press 1982.

26 J. L. Lambert, *Crime, Police and Race Relations.* OUP 1970.

27   E. Cashmore and B. Troyna, *Black Youth in Crisis* (Allen & Unwin 1982) Introduction and chapter 2.

28   R. Sykes and J. Clark, 'A Theory of Deference Exchange in Police-Civilian Encounters', *American Journal of Sociology* (1975) vol. 81 (3), pp. 584-600.

29   See Cashmore and Troyna, op. cit.

30   A similar complaint about 'bad men' theories is made in J. Q. Wilson, 'Dilemmas of Police Administration', *Public Administration Review* (1968) vol. 28, pp. 407-17.

31   Lambert, op. cit.

5

The Closed Shop and the Closed Conscience: The Churches' Failure to Argue the Moral Case

John Greenwood

Increasingly in recent years, the Church of England, along with most other Churches, has seen fit to comment on a variety of social and industrial issues. Typical of such discussions are the papers and booklets produced by the General Synod Board for Social Responsibility with its various committees.

For most of the laity it is probably no longer a matter of surprise that the hierarchy of their Church, together with its specialist advisers, should devote so much time to debating the moral aspects of work, industry, economics and employment. However, to many of us it is a matter of concern, first, that so much time and so many resources should be devoted to such debate rather than to the more obviously central aspects of our faith and, secondly, that the debate should be so one-sided. Concern for social aspects is far from unique to members of the Church of England. Writing in *Figaro,* a French Christian named Louis Pauwels complains of the Catholic Church in his country, in words roughly translated as follows:

> When I was young . . . I listened to a message which it was said was *also* social. Later, during the time of the worker priests, it was a question of a message which was *mainly* social. Now, if I am to read the French Church literature . . . I would understand that we now hear a message which is *exclusively* social.[1] (italics added)

Being himself more concerned with matters of salvation, M. Pauwels explains why for these reasons he now remains outside the Church, in the porches rather than in the main body. Those within the Church may question the point of membership of a body so exclusively concerned with social matters when politicians and others would seem better qualified to adjudicate. Those outside the Church may well draw the same conclusion.

But it is not only this pervasive preoccupation with social issues that brings a danger of the Church drawing large yawns from those remaining in the pews. It is also its one-sided approach. I would argue that on most social issues worth discussing there will be at least two opposing approaches which Christians can legitimately pursue without being accused of infidelity. My concern is with one particular issue in one particular paper, not because it is necessarily the most vital, but because it illustrates the possible diversity of views. The issue is the closed shop in industrial relations and the paper[2] seems to be typically one-sided in being an apology for closed shops. My worry is not so much with whether closed shops are a 'good thing' from the Christian point of view, whether they should be upheld, defended or ignored. Rather I am concerned for people who genuinely believe that closed shops are abhorrent or barely tolerable and who, therefore, feel increasingly isolated from a debate and a Church which seems so consistently to take no heed of their point of view.

Understanding closed shops

Publications like *Understanding Closed Shops* operate at two levels: they convince or fail to convince us by their reasoned argument *and* by their rhetoric. It is worth asking what we *feel* as we read them. We start perhaps assuming that sacking someone because they are not a union member is a fairly extreme action. Indeed we may be morally outraged at its denial of human rights. But by page four we have been soothed. Outrage and passion are apparently no longer proper dispositions for the contemporary churchman. There must always be 'facts' that can 'mitigate' 'anxieties'. We must come to 'understand' closed shops. The Foreword by the Chairman of the Industrial Committee of the General Synod Board for Social Responsibility proclaims the hope:

> that this booklet will prove to be a useful contribution to the debate on a controversial subject and that the anxieties often expressed about closed shops in British trade unionism will in some degree be mitigated by a better appreciation of the facts and the judgement which we have tried to set out here.[3]

Let us be clear. The authors do not deny that closed shops result in sacking men who have worked satisfactorily. They admit it.[4] But they do try to swamp this central fact in a mire of other secondary, often irrelevant, matters and, even more important, to defuse it, to remove its capacity to inspire moral indignation. They attempt by explaining its origins and its links with trade unionism and 'democratic' control, to make it appear normal. Is this not an odd achievement for a pamphlet whose sub-title is 'A Christian Enquiry'?

What of 'the facts and judgements' set out in the booklet itself? They are the familiar stock-in-trade of the academic discussion of industrial relations. The footnotes and reading list refer to those standard texts on this subject which would be found in typical recommended reading for students. It is arguable that this subject of industrial relations is not an academic discipline in its own right, but rather a sphere of enquiry to which a variety of established disciplines are relevant, including economics, sociology, social psychology, history and politics. While each may have established aspects of industrial relations, the subject itself has yet to be established as a systematic study. Thus, while the light shed by 'industrial relations' may be essential to 'under-standing', it is not to be treated unquestioningly. Moreover, while such study may offer insights into how closed shops develop and operate and how parties to them negotiate their existence and behave within them, it will be entirely neutral on the principal issue for Christians, which is the moral acceptability of the closed shop itself. The text of the booklet under examination, however, seems to ignore this and to proceed to muster the literature in industrial relations as an ally in its suggestion that closed shops are to be 'understood' favourably. Indeed, it seems that the booklet throughout seeks to claim a succession of allies to its cause.

Chapter 1 boldly proclaims:

There is growing support today for an increase in opportunities for employees to share in making decisions about what happens to them at work. Trade unions as a whole, too, have emerged as the chief agents of this growth towards greater shared decision-making. But how far should this process develop? The question of the closed shop, which we are examining in this Paper, is part of a wider question about how this process of joint regulation should best develop. It needs to be considered in the context of the development of trade unionism as a whole.[5]

Thus, it is suggested that the closed shop is part and parcel of normal trade unionism and that trade unionism is the motor behind the process of joint regulation of industry and industrial democracy itself. And who but Satan could be against all that?

Chapter 2 is concerned largely with the history of the development of trade unions in Britain, but not elsewhere, and reinforces the supposition that somehow the closed shop has to be understood in the context of trade unionism and its development 'as a whole'. Since this history is presented as part of a 'process of emancipation', it is hard again to see how anyone could be opposed. The same chapter draws parallels between the methods of some British trade unions in protecting their interests through closed shops and the methods of the ancient professions of the Law, Medicine and the Church.[6] And who could possibly be against all that? If this were not enough, all the other 'professions' of today, including such meritorious groups as managers, teachers and nurses, are also flocking to join unions and must, therefore, be seen to favour closed shops.

Chapter 3 is somewhat obscure. It seems to suggest that the closed shop is the very essence of the 'nature of industrial society'. People feel loyalties which drive them into closed shops and informal systems arise which must incorporate them.[7] Finally, even the hallowed name of local government democracy is invoked to prove that majorities (in closed shops) have rights to deny employment to minorities who do not wish to join trade unions.[8]

Spurious arguments

It is my contention that all these attempts to claim support for the morality of closed shops from the standpoint of trade union history, industrial sociology, or the analogy with industrial or political democracy, are entirely spurious. Instead the matter should be debated on straightforwardly moral grounds. The moral objection appears straightforward. Closed shops impose a condition of employment that all employees must be members of a trade union. The plain objection is that such unnecessary private coercion is a fundamental infringement on the rights of individuals who are compelled to join organizations to which they may not wish to belong, through the fear of losing a job or not obtaining employment. The church booklet refers to clause (2) of

Article 20 of the 1948 Universal Declaration of Human Rights which embodies this principle:

> No one may be compelled to belong to an association.[9]

However, it has to be said that this point in the booklet is reached only in Chapter 4, entitled 'Some Detailed Aspects'. Moreover, the 'aspects' treated concern such relatively narrow, specific issues as the editorial freedom of newspapers, objections to union membership on grounds of religious belief or conscience, or objections to the political activities of unions. The central, general, indeed universal issue is rather how we can possibly justify the degree of compulsion implied by closed shop agreements on individuals to join trade unions. The grounds or motives for particular groups to object to belonging to unions and paying for membership must be secondary to the fundamental question: why should anyone in a free society be obliged to join and pay for any organization to which he does not wish to belong?

For such compulsion to exist there have to be commanding reasons to override the constraints implied on freedom, as there have to be for, say, compulsory education, compulsory military service, or compulsory wearing of seat belts. Yet, even in these cases, the compulsion is normally a legal requirement laid down, in Britain, by Parliament. In the case of a closed shop the compulsion is one imposed by the union, an association, itself. The law of the country is concerned only insofar as such agreements are permitted, condoned, encouraged, restricted or banned. So there must be more potent arguments to permit people and organizations outside the usual bounds of parliamentary democracy to exercise such exclusive prerogatives.

It will not suffice simply to argue that closed shops are bound up with the nature of our present industrial system, are an integral part of the methods and history of trade unionism and are a useful means of promoting joint regulation of working life. There is nothing to prevent us changing from one method of regulation of industrial relations to another, especially if the present system involves a serious affront to the liberties of those who do not wish to join unions. It is not self-evident that joint regulation or industrial democracy are necessarily desirable means of conducting our affairs. Even if they were, they exist already in many forms throughout Europe and the world at large without compulsory union membership.

More fundamentally, it is simply false to attempt to associate the closed shop as a necessary adjunct to trade unionism itself. It is perfectly logical and legitimate to be an ardent advocate of trade unionism without being an apologist of compulsory membership. A cursory glance outside the confines of British trade unionism would reveal the closed shop to be a peculiarly Anglo-Saxon phenomenon. Elsewhere on the Continent other traditions of unionism, frequently more militant than ours, have developed in which compulsory membership is wholly alien. Far from being a phenomenon which is opposed exclusively by the enemies of unionism, it is opposed by some of its most ardent and militant representative bodies.[10]

Arguments from expediency

The booklet proclaims that the fundamental rights embodied in the 1948 Universal Declaration are:

> . . . general statements of principle to be held in proper balance with each other and with outside factors . . . It could be argued that trade unions exist primarily to try to achieve just and favourable conditions of work and protection against unemployment and that these are matters of such overwhelming importance, that they must, with mutually acceptable exceptions, outweigh the freedom not to belong to an association in particular cases.[11]

Something of this nature might have been argued to make a convincing case for compulsory trade union membership. However, even if it were so argued, it can still be held that the presumed benefits of unions either could exist without the need for closed shops or are not so valuable as to be worth the loss of freedom. There is no reference to outstanding companies like IBM whose employees flourish without any 'help' from trade unions. Moreover, while it could be argued that trade unions may exist 'to achieve just and favourable conditions of work and protection against unemployment' it is far from proved that they invariably achieve any such result. On the contrary, there is a growing literature which tends to demonstrate that, at best, unions may simply achieve more favourable conditions and better protection for their members only in the short run and at the expense of workers excluded from employment or customers who pay higher prices for inefficient output.[12]

Further expedients in favour of the closed shop are the arguments that once they exist most people accept them quite happily. Thus:

> Many companies enter into such agreements because they offer a method by which agreements negotiated with the unions refer comprehensively to all the employees concerned and tend towards the increase of order and discipline in the factory.[13]

Even if closed shops were to contribute to more orderly industrial relations, it is not clear that other less objectionable methods might not be devised to achieve the same ends. However, it is far from apparent that those sectors of industry in which closed shops predominate are havens of industrial order. As we point out later, the vast majority of closed shops in Britain are in the public sector, which has not been noted for its 'order and discipline' in recent years.

Nor is the argument that most employees do not oppose closed shops very convincing:

> . . . many people realise that the freedom of the individual can be protected by grouping together in a world of complex, large-scale, rapidly-changing organisations.[14]

Again this simply begs the question of what happens to those unfortunates who do not share this point of view. Their only hope, apparently, is that the parties to a closed shop will:

> turn a 'blind eye' to particular individuals who do not join, as is thought to be fairly widespread 'custom and practice'.[15]

Having the job on sufferance is presumably better than being unemployed.

The case of the 'free-rider' is supposed to be a powerful argument for closed shops because of:

> resentment caused by 'free-riders' who gain the advantages without accepting the obligations of membership or paying the dues . . .[16]

This familiar rhetoric begs the central question of whether unions bring long-term advantages to their members, or whether through over-manning and obstruction to new methods, unions have been a major cause in Britain's relative economic decline and record levels of unemployment. In continental Europe unions have been less restrictive and the penetration of their membership among the working population is less than here without giving rise to demands for compulsory membership. Rather, the non-members are viewed as potential recruits who must be convinced freely of the advantages of support of the unions.

Finally, it has to be said that some of the more 'sociological' reasons for 'understanding' closed shops presented in this pamphlet are the least convincing of all. One relates the existence of closed shops to some form of 'group consciousness':

> we are not talking simply of an objective legal arrangement of which we may approve or disapprove, but of something that goes much deeper into the whole history and development of the working class movement in our country.[17]

Such 'theorizing' tells us virtually nothing about the nature of closed shops and still less of the justice of their existence. Such pseudo-Marxist appeals to the depths of the history and development of the working class movement and its consciousness should be resisted. It is really less than intellectually honest to imply that anyone opposed to closed shops cannot understand or sympathize with the deeper concerns of the working classes. If this were to be accepted, large numbers of people will simply be excluded from discussing the matter altogether. The fact remains that closed shops are arrangements to which some people object for reasons no less serious or profound than anything to do with the group consciousness of those who favour such arrangements. It may be true that closed shops only come into existence:

> after a group of work people, albeit informally, have recognised that a closed shop will help them to regulate their working environment. It is shop floor pressure which, it is claimed here, initially brings a closed shop into existence.[18]

But may we ask what is to happen to those who do not 'recognise' that the closed shop will regulate their working environment in an ideal fashion? And, back to the fundamental question: is such 'shop-floor pressure' legitimate or acceptable?

Nor is it convincing to suggest that the closed shop is an

inevitable part of our system of industrial relations or, more grandly, of 'the nature of industrial society'[19] itself. Chapter 3 argues a point made from the time of the Donovan Commission on Trade Unions and Employers' Associations in 1968 concerning the existence in Britain of both a formal system of industrial relations and an informal system. The details of such a distinction need not concern us. It may or may not be a useful means of analysing the nature of our industrial relations. What needs to be argued is not whether an informal system exists or whether closed shops should be seen as part of such an informal system, but whether any particular system should be made compulsory.

The unacceptable face of trade unionism

Somehow the right not to join a trade union if a person so chooses is not to be placed on the same level as the right of others to join unions if they choose differently.[20] Nothing in this pamphlet has convinced me that this is justified. Nothing has led me to change my view that the right not to join organizations is fundamental to a free society as is widely accepted in the practice and law of most other countries. In particular, I have sought to question the following kinds of argument:

1   Closed shops give people a chance to share in joint regulation of working life. (There are other means of achieving the same end if so desired.)
2   Closed shops are an integral part of trade unionism and its history in Britain. (It is presumably possible to change future 'history' if desired.)
3   Non-members of unions are resented. (It is for the unions to convince workers to join without the need for compulsion.)
4   Most employers are happy to accept them. (Some employers are not.)
5   They would not exist unless groups had pressed for them. (Some employees may still not be happy with such arrangements.)
6   Closed shops are an integral part of our system of industrial relations. (This can be changed.)

The grounds on which a case must be made are moral grounds, since the basic objection is a moral one. It is dismaying, therefore, that the Church should devote so much time and effort to other criteria and pretexts. Furthermore, it is disappointing that attention should not be given to other objections to the closed shop.

Both trade unions and closed shops provide a degree of power to their members and officials which needs to be exercised responsibly. In particular, justice requires that the powers of officials be exercised according to the wishes of their members. Justice also requires that the exercise of union power be limited to the extent that other people — non-members, consumers, the public at large, members of other unions — should not be made to suffer unduly as a result. In recent years a growing majority of the public believes the balance of power is tilted unduly in favour of the unions and needs to be reformed by law. The closed shop is central to this debate because it gives the unions and their officials an assurance of not losing membership if their policies are unpopular, and of compelling reluctant workers to strike on pain of losing their union card and hence their jobs.

One author reveals:

> Of the 2.3 million workers who joined closed shops between 1962 and 1978, 74 per cent were in the nationalised industries.[21]

As he points out, the fact that many nationalized industries themselves represent trading monopolies gives double cause for concern that they should conscript employees into closed shops. In the event of a strike, the public can be deprived of an essential service without recourse to alternatives, while in the absence of strike ballots or other democratic procedures, the union is assured of blind support because anyone defying the union can be sacked. However, even this kind of abuse is not the worst problem. A closed shop can give union officials power over who is to be employed by a firm and even for whom, or with whom, the firm's employees will be prepared to work. Such powers can be exercised in an arbitrary, political fashion, or can be quite simply corrupt. In the extreme case of newspapers, customers or employers may be forced to administer bribes to obtain supplies and the prospective employee may be obliged to buy his job.

Whatever church apologists may think, it is more significant that opinion polls show most union members are opposed to the abuse of union power, and its principle buttress in the closed shop. Once again we find the Church so anxious to bend to popular — or vocal — opinion, only to find itself on the wrong side. In the process it offends many of its own (voluntary) members without attracting fresh support for its secular gospel.

NOTES

1 Louis Pauwels, 'Dieu a-t-il lu ce sondage?', *Le Figaro*, 9 April 1983.

2 Church Information Office, *Understanding Closed Shops: A Christian Enquiry into Compulsory Trade Union Membership*, Ludo Press 1977.

3 ibid., Foreword.

4 ibid., Introduction.

5 ibid., p. 3.

6 ibid., p. 10.

7 ibid., pp. 12-14.

8 ibid., p. 16.

9 ibid., p. 21.

10 For example, the Communist-led Confédération Général du Travail in France and equivalent C.G.I.L. in Italy.

11 Church Information Office, ibid., p. 22.

12 e.g. Lord Robbins *et al.*, *Trade Unions: Public Goods or Public 'Bads'*, IEA 1978; F. A. Hayek, *Unemployment and the Unions*, IEA 1980.

13 Church Information Office, ibid., p. 5.

14 ibid., p. 5.

15 ibid., p. 4.

16 ibid., p. 5.

17 ibid., p. 3.

18 ibid., pp. 2-3.

19 ibid., ch. 3.

20 ibid., p. 15.

21 Parry Rogers, 'Public Sector Workers: A Clear Case For Treatment', *The Director*, April 1983.

6

Racism:
Neither a Sin Apart nor an Excuse for Hysteria

Dennis O'Keeffe

Introduction

Racism in British Society, a publication by the Catholic Commission for Racial Justice (CCRJ)[1] typifies two widespread features of contemporary discussions of racism. First, it is conceptually sloppy and confused. Second, its charge that Great Britain is characterized by general and institutional racial hatred and discrimination is a gross slander on British society.

This chapter briefly examines the document's errors or confusions on the following topics: the concept of race itself; the connections between race and culture; definitions of racism; the mental framework of racism; types of racism and discrimination; and finally, the means of combating racism.

The concept of race

Racism in British Society opens with a jejune account of the notorious difficulties of the concept of race. It points out that some people hold that 'race' does not exist (p. 1), a curious observation in a publication which is predicated on the view that 'racism' does exist. In its casual remarks on the randomness and variability of racial characteristics, the report loses sight of the sociological commonplace that what is perceived as 'real' is real in its consequences. Having noted the uncertain character of racial differences the report then opines on p. 2 as follows:

> Furthermore, and most importantly, there is no evidence that more fundamental human characteristics (such as intelligence, character, or physical dexterity) correspond to 'racial differences'.

What is of interest here is the eagerness to foreclose the question. Not for the authors 'it is unlikely' or 'research has failed to find significant correspondence between race and intelligence', but 'there is no evidence', indeed, 'most importantly there is no evidence'. Are the authors of that tendency which is sure there never could be and would stop any further research? It is just not clear what purpose this ringing denial of any interracial differences in 'intelligence, character or physical dexterity' is meant to serve. Does the report fear that evidence that such differences occur, would, if it could be established, imply the establishment of a grisly polity on the lines of apartheid? This is not, in fact, the case. There are enormous difficulties in conceptualizing, measuring and explaining putative phenomena such as intelligence. Such difficulties are compounded beyond measure in the case of inter-group comparisons where the groups concerned have widely different historical, cultural and social experiences. However, if it *were* possible to establish such variations they would have no inevitable political implications. If *on average* people of Chinese extraction were shown to be more 'intelligent' than people of Anglo-Saxon origin, there would be *no case* for arguing that the two groups should not intermarry, live in proximity, attend the same schools, do the same jobs.

It is quite false to treat attempts to discover whether there may be interracial variations in intelligence as proto-Nazi in tendency.[2] However much or little substance there may be in such work it is surely the orchestrated cry that it must be worthless or racist that is the real intolerance.

Race and culture

The report notes that race and culture are distinct, the former a matter of genes, the latter 'a social rather than a biological legacy' (p. 2). There is no such thing as superior or inferior races. The issue of culture is more problematic:

> However, the question remains as to whether some cultures can be said to be superior to others . . . ethnocentric attitudes (the belief that one's own culture is superior to other cultures) are closely related to racist attitudes. While racism assumes superior and inferior races, ethnocentrism assumes superior and inferior cultures. The two often reinforce one another (p. 2).

Despite the modification offered by the final adverb 'often' the tendency in this paragraph is gravely misleading. The coupling of cultural and racial attitudes here is far too glib. It is perfectly possible to believe in the superiority of a given culture without drawing any racial conclusions from this. This is a commonplace French attitude, for example. It is also possible for people who are not much removed from each other culturally to dislike each other on grounds of race, e.g. some whites and some blacks in the Anglo-Saxon countries. But more than this, it is not at all obvious that either racial *or* cultural antipathy necessarily involves notions of superiority or inferiority. It may be so, and is a matter for empirical enquiry. *A priori* I would maintain that an indispensable ingredient of such antipathy is hostility to perceived differences.

The report, however, moves on to a discussion which effectively puts questions of assumed superiority or inferiority at the heart of the matter:

> Any attempt to judge one's own culture superior to others faces an initial fundamental difficulty, for the judgement is made from within one's own culture. A westerner attempting to judge the relative values of different cultures would be likely to use western values (p. 2).

Here the tired old work-horse of cultural relativism has been dragged out of his retirement stable once more. What, for example, is the origin of the view that racial prejudice is immoral and unjustifiable? The answer is: precisely those modern 'western' values which the report is questioning. Interestingly enough, the report *nowhere* mentions that anti-racism is a product of liberalism. But the weakness in the case can be much more glaringly revealed through an invented quotation of our own:

> Nazi practices cannot be justly attacked from the viewpoint of western democracy.

For 'Nazi practices' we could substitute 'feet-binding', 'slavery', 'female circumcision', 'droit de seigneur' and any number of horrors to reveal the essential absurdity of cultural relativism, which is in any case contrary to the Christian viewpoint that moral improvement is achievable.

The report goes on to ask how important it is to be the first to arrive at a particular cultural achievement (p. 2), a question so odd that one is, initially, at a loss to know how to respond. The question is followed by an even stranger one:

> Who should get credit when a particular culture reaches a peak of achievement in a given area? (p. 2).

The answer, apparently, is that no one should. All achievements are built on prior achievements. Michel Leiris is quoted to the effect that algebra comes to us from the Arabs (Leiris omits to say that it is of Indian provenance), astronomy from the Chaldeans, coffee from Ethiopia, tea and silk from China, maize, tobacco and the potato from the Americas, etc. On page 3 we learn that the 'miracle of Greece' was really somebody else's miracle.

The unspoken assumption behind this historical belittlement would seem to be that intellectual and technical history which celebrates the achievements of any particular society is necessarily racist and/or ethnocentric. This is quite false. For example it is a very important issue in general economic and political history to explore how and why industrial capitalism or parliamentary democracy emerged. For those who believe that they have bestowed enormous benefits on a still too limited part of the world's population, the crucial question is not who invented them but *how they can be disseminated*. Yet if the major issue of the worthwhileness of an innovation is granted then there would seem little reason to deny the more minor issue of national credit. If the invention of writing was important, why should the ancient cultures of Sumeria and Egypt not be acclaimed for it?

It is precisely the view that particular civilizations are worthy of praise which the report is castigating. A society may be indicted for moral failure, it seems, but not acclaimed for its successes:

> Because of the difficulty of finding an objective vantage point from which to judge various cultures, because of the intrinsic connection of different cultures in which they contribute to one another's achievements, because of the development of a culture over centuries and through complex stages of progress and decline, and finally because of the complicated variety of value judgements that would be entailed, *a generalisation about the superiority of one culture over another is not possible* (p. 3, italics in original text).

The absurd *non sequitur* with which this extract ends can be mercilessly ridiculed, again, if we substitute for the italicized clause the words:

> a generalization about the superiority of democracy over Hitlerism or Stalinism is not possible.

The report's treatment of culture combines a probably erroneous assumption with a definitely false conclusion. From the undemonstrated view that questions of inferiority and superiority are intrinsic to cultural and racial prejudice, it moves to the crazy notion that one culture cannot be regarded as superior to another. Historical achievement can be dismissed by reference to its antecedents. Moral shortcomings in a society are not, interestingly, to be exonerated by any comparable historical relativization. It is passing strange that a soi-disant Christian document should take so odd and asymmetrical a view of the very heart of human consolation — the doctrine of redemption and improvement. Historical empathy for cannibalism and the burning of widows; jeremiads for the racist British: it is extraordinary that the report does not observe the contradiction.

Definitions of racism

The report is no better when it comes to defining racism. It starts with a curious assault on demotic speech. It is apparently illegitimate to refer to people's having British or Irish 'blood' (p. 3). A man of Asian parentage born here is, so it seems, not 'Asian'. Have British Chinese or Indians been consulted about this extraordinary pronouncement? If we are to ban all metaphors such as 'blood' will we not rapidly denude our language? There then follows this sentence:

> If one looks at racism in terms of its effects it matters little whether it is intentional or unintentional or whether or not it is based on racist ideas or prejudices (p. 3).

This is, in fact, two statements. The first is false. Deliberate wickedness is clearly worse than unintentional bad behaviour. The second statement is, strictly speaking, nonsense. The notion of racism without racial prejudice has the logical status of gluttony without gluttons or murder without murderous intent. This, however, is what the document does indeed hold. If black people end up with the worst housing in an area, as a result of allocation by criteria not intended as racist, racism is at work (p. 3). This is not genuine analysis. It is promiscuous moral agonizing since it implies that any racial group not reaching some approved mean in housing, jobs, 'O' Levels or any other index of achievement, is somehow being subjected to racist discrimination. The logical drift of this approach is towards the nightmarish chimera of literal equality in the distribution of all desirable goods.

Three definitions of racism are then offered, each seen as only partly valid, but all three taken as useful together:

1 belief in the superiority of a particular race; theory that human abilities are determined by race;
2 a pattern of behaviour whose consequences, intended or not, are to reinforce present (racial) inequalities;
3 racism is prejudice plus power.

The report holds that (1) is inadequate through saying nothing about practices. Though the text seems already to have accepted (2), it is now rebuked for saying nothing about attitudes. The limitation of (3) on the other hand, is, apparently, its view that ideas and practices are racist only in conjunction with other phenomena. At the same time it is pointed out how useful many people have found this third definition. What is not observed is its extreme weakness. The most virulent prejudice is to be found amongst relatively poor and powerless people — poor whites in the USA and the lumpen-proletariat of the British National Front. There may well also be violent hatred of white people amongst politically feeble black people, a point unlikely to be raised in a report which identifies racial prejudice exclusively with *white* people.

The mental framework of racism

A sketch etiology of modern racism is now attempted (p. 4). Tenuously relevant accounts of biblical racial prejudice and of the impact of the nineteenth-century work of the Count de Gobineau accompany a *correct* identification of the connection between racial prejudice and the rise of European imperialism and the slave trade. There is, however, a misleading identification of racial prejudice with the emergence of industrial capitalism. As Milton Friedman has pointed out, the secular trend of capitalist markets is towards the eradication of prejudices against minorities.[3]

The tone of these paragraphs is generally neo-Marxist. The dynamics of self-reforming European colonialism are not considered. It is not mentioned that Europeans *abolished* slavery, that it was endemic in Africa among Africans, that it continues there to the very present. Instead there are sneers at the white man's burden and, extraordinarily, an apparent rejection of 'popular notions of Christian mission'. Is not Christianity true, and are not all other faiths, however magnificent, in crucial senses false? If this is not the case what is the point of Christianity?

There follows a discussion of stereotypes and scapegoats of elephantine obviousness, once again basically aimed, however, at establishing the false proposition that there is no such thing as 'primitiveness'. Given that this conclusion would seem to imply that no social arrangements prior to our own can be reckoned as having been in need of improvement, one is at a loss to know why the report is so concerned to improve ours.

This section concludes that in our society racist attacks are alarmingly common (though whether these include attacks by black muggers on non-blacks is not considered) but suggests that the more ordinary form of racist behaviour is discrimination (p. 5).

Discrimination

The CCRJ holds that there is widespread intentional discrimination against non-whites in the matter of employment (p. 6). Here one would expect the report to be on strong ground. So insistent have the cries been over the years that I had always assumed that, despite my own experience of black and Asian doctors, dentists (my own), lawyers, bank clerks, bus-drivers etc., the charges must be true. My suspicions were aroused, however, by the fact that the sole study of unambiguous employer bias the report notes was for Nottingham (not London or Birmingham) between 1977 and 1979. Of a tiny valid sample of 100 cases, less than half show employer bias against non-white recruits. If the phenomenon *is* widespread, can we not expect some more impressive evidence?

The report then turns to a British Leyland case where the *origin* of discrimination against *one* black recruit was a shop-floor meeting of the AUEW. The management is rightly castigated for falling in with this, but the union, oddly, is not indicted. Is there some ideological wire-crossing here? It is not obvious that the racial prejudices of organized labour are more excusable than those of capital.

The report then deals with 'unintentional' racism. The example cited is of a South London firm which used to recruit its van drivers mostly by recommendation of existing drivers. Since all forty-five of these were white, it suggested evidence of direct discrimination. The CCRJ held that in multi-racial labour markets word of mouth recruitment should not be used. During the investigation the company did, in fact, hire two black drivers.

Two comments seem appropriate. First, word of mouth hiring practices cannot be called 'racist' except in the most morally exiguous sense of the term. Second, the kind of quota rigging that seems to be proposed here is very sinister in potential. Should we, by extension, require the dismissal of members of over-represented minorities from certain activities such as catering and cleaning at Heathrow Airport? Should there be quotas *preventing* as well as permitting access to certain occupations?

Institutional racism

The report finds in the history of British immigration legislation over the last twenty years clear evidence of institutional racism (p. 7). What is unacceptable in this position is the undemocratic view that it is wrong for the majority population of a community to prefer and seek to perpetuate its own majority. In fact the opposite is true. In a democracy it is governments who should require very strong reasons to defy majority opinion. Neither is it reasonable to confuse national, racial or cultural preferences with the kind of hatred and intolerance implied usually by the term 'racism'. If there were a Caribbean island to which people of different races wished to move in large numbers, would its citizens be 'racist' if they sought to favour the entry of those most like them in appearance and/or culture?

The report now moves on (pp. 7-9) to an examination of housing. It finds that council housing allocation, building society practices and the policies of accommodation agencies constitute institutional racism at the three levels of council houses, owner-occupancy and private renting (p. 9). The possibility that in early decades newcomers would be expected to do less well than the established population is not considered. Neither is it fair to indict councils since the report itself makes it clear that they do not deliberately set out to disadvantage anyone. No credit is given to successive governments for their attempts to combat landlord bias. No consideration is given to the possibility that non-whites may be higher than average mortgage risks.

Finally the report in these pages is cavalier in its terminology. Are Pakistanis and Indians 'blacks'? Are Chinese? Certainly the document slides into a catch-all 'blacks' to describe immigrants to this country and their children (p. 9). Perhaps these people might resent being herded together for the Commission's convenience.

Combating racism

The CCRJ wants legislation against racism to be wider in scope than what is permitted by the 1976 Race Relations Act. The report looks wistfully at the United States with its much more extensive networks of affirmative action (pp. 10-11). Its authors seem not to be aware of the literature in the United States to the effect that most interventionist programmes of this kind are both costly and ineffective, or worse, counterproductive, as George Gilder argues.[4] This easy administrative optimism stands in the sharpest contrast to the grotesque pessimism about the attitudes of white people:

> This resistance among white people is so fundamental that it is doubtful whether any effective anti-racist education can take place which does not take such resistance into account (p. 10).

Yet the report acknowledges that there are possibilities for improvement. Schools are praised for their attempts to mount a critique of racist and ethnocentric attitudes and to develop a multiracial curriculum (p. 10). No mention is made of the hostility now being voiced in many quarters, including black teachers and educationalists, to innovations such as Black Studies.[5] However, the report holds that, though it is too early to evaluate them, 'racism awareness courses' may prove salutary. The commendable thing about these Maoist-sounding exercises is, it seems, that they are 'specifically designed to reach deeper attitudinal levels' (p. 11).

The report concludes with the profoundly socialistic view that what is needed is more intervention. More funds, more laws, more programmes (p. 12) are the way to improvement. The intractable evidence accumulated in the twentieth century, to the effect that the problems of the human situation admit of no easy administrative solution, is simply not taken into account.

Commentary

The spirit of criticism is essential to a free and creative society. *Racism in British Society* moves beyond criticism. It is an exercise in self-denigration, an example of the very worst sort of confused moral agonizing. It does not helpfully identify the *nature* of racial or cultural prejudice and yet it proceeds to accuse virtually the whole indigenous nation of them. No sane individual would deny that many people in our society have prejudices against people of different race from themselves. Neither is such prejudice confined to white people as the report (by omission) suggests.

The report falls in with the sub-Marxist convention that racial prejudice is an immorality apart, dwarfing other sins. It is not. Like other forms of human folly, racial prejudice may be mild or murderous. Nowhere does *Racism in British Society* consider the possibility that racial prejudice in this country is typically mild rather than extreme. This might well be the case in a country which has absorbed some three million non-whites in a few decades with remarkably little violence. It cannot be discussed, however, by a Commission putting its trust in the socialist solution to the problems of the human condition, namely the vast expansion of the state.

Nowhere does the report consider the central contradiction in the camp of all those who claim that our society is pervasively racist in character. If it were so, would so many non-whites stay? Would so many want to come?

It *is* important that Catholics should try to understand and help ethnic minorities. It is precisely because this sort of document makes no serious effort to understand racial and cultural issues in all their complexity, substituting a stylized sub-Marxist tirade for genuine discussion, that it will do a disservice to the very people it would claim to want to help.

NOTES

1 The Catholic Commission for Racial Justice is not the official voice of the Roman Catholic church in this country on matters of race. I have no

way of knowing how far the bishops agree with the CCRJ. Neither do I know who or how many people wrote *Racism in British Society*.

2   A. Flew, *Sociology, Equality and Education* (Macmillan 1976) pp. 62-76.
3   M. Friedman, *Capitalism and Freedom* (University of Chicago Press 1962) p. 21.
4   G. Gilder, *Wealth and Poverty*. Basic Books 1981.
5   M. Stone, *The Education of the Black Child in Britain*. Fontana 1981.

7

Unemployment:
Putting Faith in the New Princes

Robert Miller

Some 'Christian' counsel

If we are to develop a response to the problems of unemployment which face us today, we need to pay attention to the experience of those who have gone before us and to build on the work they have done . . . We see the importance of intervening in the organisation and structure of the social order. We see the importance also of developing alternatives that will profoundly affect the workings of the dominant industrial and social aspects of that order.[1]

Unemployment has always been an important political issue . . . The policy of the present Government is based on the philosophy that if people help themselves they will help the community as a whole, and if the market is left to get on with minimum interference from outside, things will come right . . . The way back to jobs is via commercial efficiency in the private enterprise system.
Few people now believe this is working. (italics added)[2]

Economic growth can be stimulated by the Government spending more money directly on its own projects, through its own departments, local authorities, nationalised industries and public utilities.
The gain from this sort of economic growth accrues mainly to the unemployed who find work and to the future through investment in long-lasting national capital assets.[3]

Contact unemployed people sensitively and help them to tell you what it is like to be out of work.
Take political action: join an unemployment march; take your Church banner with you; write to your MP, MEP or to the Prime Minister.[4]

'Doing something about it'

The Churches are frequently tormented by the assumption that they ought to do (or at least say) something about 'unemployment', and this has led to a multiplicity of books and papers on the subject. The Churches are resolved that there should be a Christian contribution to the public discussion of remedies for unemployment. But it is here that the difficulties begin. Having convinced themselves on theological grounds that work is good and consequently that unemployment is a social evil which is implicitly condemned by Scripture and tradition, they feel that they must articulate some Christian 'response' to the problem. But with rare exceptions, the means they propose for reducing unemployment are interventionist. Unemployment, according to the Churches, can be reduced only by state intervention whether by work schemes or outright reflation.

From unexceptional theology to dubious economics

There is no reason to object to the theology on which the Churches base their concern for the unemployed. Many writers point to St Thomas Aquinas and the doctrine that work is essential for the fulfillment of man's God-given potential.[5] Work, they point out, is a way of sharing in the creation, though they tend to forget that in this sense, work is more than labour for wages and should include the activities of the self-employed, managers, businessmen and entrepreneurs.[6] From the assertion of the evils of unemployment, the leap to an interventionist cure is frequently made without more ado. In many cases, this seems less an attempt to connect incarnational theology with collectivist means than a very limited view of economic theory. The writers have not appreciated the possibility that intervention may actually have helped cause unemployment, tends to perpetuate it, and that the most successful way to reduce it may be to diminish the extensive intervention already imposed by government.

An interesting example of this slide from unexceptional theology to questionable economics can be found in the Bishop of Liverpool's book, *Bias to the Poor*:

> It is precisely the arbitrary nature of the market which means that it must not be our sole master. At present the market does not need the labour of 30 per cent of the labour force in many areas of Merseyside and many other cities in the developed countries.[7]

The Bishop makes the wholly unexamined assumption, unsupported by theological or economic argument, that it is 'the market' which causes and perpetuates unemployment. The truth is that the causes of unemployment are a technical matter where the Church and the Bishop have no special competence. The Bishop makes no attempt to come to terms with economists such as Professor Patrick Minford of Liverpool University who ascribes unemployment to, amongst other things, a combination of trade union wage-fixing, minimum wage regulation and social security incomes which are high relative to net incomes from work.[8]

In identifying the most effective *policy* for the permanent reduction of unemployment, the Churches can have no special authority or expertise and their spokesmen write and speak as amateurs. This verdict can be illustrated by an analogy with medicine. If Christianity has something to say about the social order and policy towards unemployment, we might agree that it is in a similar position with regard to medicine. It is legitimate for the Church to argue that society pays insufficient regard to the needs of the sick, but we would be amazed if the Church instructed doctors in the details of treatment of their patients on theological grounds. Similarly, we may feel surprised that the Church should presume to pontificate on the best means of reducing unemployment. Given a stated end, the means is a matter for competent experts who may or may not agree on the best course of action. It is difficult to see how the Church can avoid saying anything which is not either platitudinous or little different from that coming from a secular source. One of the striking features of the church statements on unemployment is that they are so little different from those of any other group of well-intentioned people. This is well illustrated by the statement of the Bishop of Liverpool quoted above. Despite claims that a specifically Christian 'input' or 'leavening' is necessary, the values and prescriptions expressed in most statements on unemployment by churchmen are almost identical to those of socialist politicians. This being the case, one wonders that the Churches deploy their carefully husbanded resources in areas where they seem to say nothing very different from other interested people rather than where they are qualified to make a distinctive contribution.

Temple, economic technique and Christian values

The view that while ends may be a legitimate subject for comment by churchmen, the means adopted by politicians to achieve those ends were not — the doctrine of the 'autonomy of technique'[9] — has been attacked. The economist Charles Elliott wrote:

> Any kind of social science, whether it be sociology or economics or planning or politics, has hidden within it a whole range of value judgements. Consider the trade-off between equality and efficiency. Put that policy in the context of a pay policy. At what point is it 'right' to forgo equality in order to increase efficiency? There is no unique solution which arises inevitably from economic logic. Different economists will solve that problem in different ways according to their own value systems. It is, therefore, no genuine solution to the problem that Temple identified to call in the expert and leave him to produce a value free solution.[10]

In other words, since most 'technical' problems in economics involve value judgements, such questions cannot be left to the expert and are the legitimate concern of the Church.

Such a view exaggerates the difficulty of disentangling the value judgements from the economic prescriptions and overstates the number of occasions where Christianity requires a specific economic judgement. Charles Elliott assumes that because value judgements are involved, it follows that the Church must have a single distinctive view. But even suppose we accept Canon Mascall's view (which he contrasts with E. R. Norman's): 'If . . . one really believes in the Christian doctrines of Creation, Incarnation and Redemption . . . one has a criterion by which one can, and must, bring all political and social considerations under judgement',[11] it does not follow that 'being under judgement' means that there is only one method of achieving a particular end acceptable to all Christians.

The suggestion that technique cannot be 'autonomous', can be made to produce ridiculous conclusions. Does the Church really condemn an economist such as Professor Minford who believes that unemployment can be reduced permanently only by eliminating wage fixing in the labour market, reducing the taxation of low incomes and the disparity between incomes in and out of work.[12] Professor Minford may be mistaken, but it is difficult to see how the Church can condemn him on theological grounds, since he is certainly seeking the same end as the Churches — the reduction of unemployment.

It might be argued that Christianity rules out the solution of economic problems by means of markets, on the grounds that they conflict with the early Christian emphasis on 'koinonia' — the common life of love and sharing.[13] But the same difficulty appears again; it seems likely that 'koinonia' is best promoted by social institutions which include free markets rather than the bureaucratic and collectivist alternative. How best to promote 'koinonia' is itself in part a technical question involving more than the common superficial equation of markets with the law of the jungle.

Fallible governments

The limited theoretical diet of churchmen concerning the economics of unemployment is exemplified by their apparent ignorance of the development in recent decades of the theory of 'public choice' or the 'economics of politics', or even the earlier 'monetarist' criticisms of Keynesian interventionism. The 'public choice' economists have applied the economic theory of markets to democratic governments and bureaucracies. The analysis has been used to show that governments are as likely to 'fail' as markets and consequently that appeals to government intervention to cure defects in markets involve highly optimistic assumptions about the role of government in economic affairs.[14] The basic assumptions of the theory of 'public choice' should be grasped easily by churchmen, as they can be seen as another aspect of the Christian doctrine of original sin.

Previously, economists in the Keynesian tradition who still seem to dominate the economic thinking of the Churches, had taken a highly optimistic view of human nature as it is found in governments and bureaucracies. One exponent of the economics of politics described the assumptions in the following way:

> Keynes hoped for a world where monetary and fiscal policy, carried out by wise men in authority, could ensure conditions of prosperity, equity, freedom, and possibly peace . . .[15]

Keynes' biographer, R. F. Harrod, described Keynes' views similarly:

> We have seen that he [Keynes] was strongly involved with what I have called the presuppositions of the Harvey Road. One of these presuppositions may perhaps be summarised in the idea that the government of Britain was and could continue to be in the hands of an intellectual aristocracy using the method of persuasion.

Harrod went on:

> Keynes tended till the end to think of the really important decisions being reached by a small group of intelligent people, like that fashioning the Bretton Woods plan.[16]

These optimistic assumptions about human nature have characterized the neo-Keynesian mismanagement of the economy and have been an essential part of the system of 'demand stabilization' which was intended to avoid the cycle of recurrent slump and boom. Such a system of intervention is still advocated by many churchmen to cure or at least to reduce the present unemployment. Yet the criticism of these assumptions by the exponents of 'public choice' theory seems to coincide closely with orthodox Christianity. Both would accept that politicians and bureaucrats have motives very similar to those of ordinary people. In other words, both theologians and 'public choice' economists believe that those entrusted with economic management are likely to be fallible in virtue and knowledge. In contrast, the Keynesian recipe is founded on the fallacy of what one Christian writer has called 'angelism'.[17]

According to St Thomas Aquinas, the fall has disordered human nature, so that it is subject to four 'wounds': lust, ignorance, weakness of will and malevolence.[18] Whilst the first and last 'wounds' no doubt exist in most politicians and bureaucrats they do not appear to be of special significance in the formation of economic policy. Ignorance is of prime importance, as Milton Friedman and Hayek have pointed out; our knowledge of the economy is such that it is impossible to know when and to what degree macroeconomic discretionary intervention is desirable.[19] For example, it may be that at the point of recovery a government injects purchasing power into the economy with the effect of producing a highly destabilizing surge in demand which may cause an even larger recession at a later date. According to the interventionist theory, the 'reflation' should take place as the economy enters a recession, but in practice this is extraordinarily difficult to judge and any mistake will simply intensify instability.

Weakness of will can also be exemplified with ease in the management of the economy under the neo-Keynesian dispensation. It was argued originally that stability in purchasing power and employment could be maintained by ensuring that the government's deficit balanced over the period of the business cycle. The budget would be allowed to go into deficit during the downward phase of the cycle with a surplus being achieved in the boom, thereby stabilizing purchasing power and employment. Unfortunately this has not been the experience of either Britain or America since the 'Keynesian Revolution'[20] destroyed the 'old time fiscal religion' of annual balanced budgets and led to more or less continuous over-stimulation which is always more attractive in the short term to both politicians and electors.

The reason for this fall from the ideal was pointed out by the 'public choice' economists. Since we are not ruled by a virtuous élite, we have had to rely on ordinary fallible party politicians. In the words of Professors Buchanan and Wagner:

> The economy is not controlled by the sages of Harvey Road [where Keynes lived in Cambridge], but by politicians engaged in a continuing competition for office. The political decision structure is entirely different from that which was envisaged by Keynes himself, and it is out of this starkly different political setting that the Keynesian norms have been applied with destructive results. Political decisions in the United States are made by elected politicians, who respond to the desires of voters or the ensconced bureaucracy.[21]

This backsliding by politicians explains why intervention has proven so one-sided. Politicians tend to use their office to assemble coalitions of supporters by carefully dispensing the proceeds of taxation and borrowing. The tendency is thus for public spending to increase as those who benefit immediately recognize the origin of their advantage and those harmed by taxation are so widely distributed or so few in numbers that they have no electoral significance. The temptation is to defer the necessary taxation by borrowing, thereby giving rise to a series of budget deficits. As

79

Buchanan and Wagner put it: it creates or increases 'a deficit, a reduction in real tax rates, an increase in real rates of public spending, or some combination of the two. In any event, there are direct and immediate gainers and no losers.'[22] In turn a series of budget deficits increases the likelihood of an expansion of the money supply and consequently of inflation. But inflation increases economic instability and introduces structural distortions into the economy which are an important cause of unemployment. Without the restriction of a balanced budget rule the natural tendency of politicians in a democracy is to perpetuate instability and unemployment as the price of electoral support.

The 'public choice' economists provide a ready explanation for the inflation, instability and unemployment of the last two decades which coincides with the consequences of the 'wounds' of ignorance and weakness of will which derive from the fall. They suggest that a return to large scale interventionism as a cure for unemployment would be likely to increase economic instability and do nothing to effect a permanent reduction in unemployment.

The unbalanced economic diet of the Church

The Churches' 'contribution' to the discussion of the problem of unemployment has been marked by a highly restricted diet of economic theory. They have wholly ignored the development of new theories of 'public choice' which seem to fit naturally with the traditional doctrine of original sin. Fallen man, whether politician or bureaucrat, cannot fulfil the expectations of economists who claim that unemployment and economic instability can be reduced by judicious intervention. Politicians cannot know when they ought to act and only rarely will they have the strength of character to intervene in the way theory requires. The Churches would be on firmer ground if they stopped assuming that social evils can always be cured by intervention and that politicians somehow escaped the fall or have recovered the perfection of Eden.

NOTES

1   *Work or What? A Christian Examination of the Employment Crisis,* an ecumenical group of the BCC (CIO 1977) p. 37.

2   Paul Brett, *Unemployment and the Future of Work,* Church of England General Synod Board for Social Responsibility Industrial and Economic Committee, Working Paper 14 (1982) Section 2, p. 3.

3   Bob Jackson, *Government Economic Policy and Concern for My Neighbour,* Grove Pastoral Series, no. 12 (1982) pp. 11-12.

4   Paul Brett, op. cit., section 7, p. 1 and section 7, p. 3.

5   Paul Brett, op. cit., section 5, p. 6.

6   There is a striking parallel between the traditional theological accounts of how God freely created the universe *ex nihilo* and the description of creation of new goods and products by entrepreneurs by economists of the 'Austrian' school of subjectivist economists — such as von Mises, Hayek, Israel Kirzner and G. L. S. Shackle. Aquinas gives the impression of being an 'Austrian' theologian.

7   David Sheppard, *Bias to the Poor* (Hodder & Stoughton 1983) p. 137.

8   Patrick Minford, David Davies, Michael Peel and Alison Sprague, *Unemployment – Cause and Cure.* Martin Robertson 1983. The Bishop's ignorance is surprising as all the authors are members of the Department of Economic and Business Studies at Liverpool University.

9   William Temple, *Christianity and Social Order* (Shepheard-Walwyn, SPCK 1976, 1st edn 1942) pp. 40ff. Temple illustrated the distinction very clearly in the following statement:

> At the end of this book I shall offer, in my capacity as a Christian citizen, certain proposals for definite action which would, in my private judgement, conduce to a more Christian ordering of society; but if any member of the Convocation of York be so ill-advised as to table a resolution that these proposals be adopted as a political programme for the Church, I should in my capacity as Archbishop resist that proposal with all my force, and should probably, as President of the Convocation, rule it out of order (p. 41).

10 Charles Elliott, 'Vision and Utopia', *Theology*, May 1978, quoted in G. S. Ecclestone, *The Church of England and Politics*, General Synod Board for Social Responsibility (1981) pp. 48-9.

11 E. L. Mascall, 'Christianity Reinterpreted and Politicised: the Thesis Examined', in *Christianity Reinterpreted? A Critical Re-examination of the 1978 Reith Lectures*, ed. Kenneth Leech, Jubilee Lent Lectures for 1979 (The Jubilee Group in association with the Church in Wales Publications 1982) p. 6.

12 Patrick Minford, *The Problem of Unemployment,* Selsdon Group Policy Series no. 5 (1981) pp. 13ff.

13 Kenneth Leech, 'The Theology of Dr. Norman', in *Christianity Reinterpreted,* op. cit., p. 56.

14 This optimistic view was not shared by their classical predecessors. Professor T. W. Hutchison has pointed out that the classical economists had a much more realistic view of politicians. T. W. Hutchison, 'The

Market Economy and the Franchise', in *The Politics and Philosophy of Economics* (Basil Blackwell 1981).

15 Arthur Smithies, 'Reflections on the Work and Influence of John Maynard Keynes', *Quarterly Journal of Economics,* November 1951.

16 R. F. Harrod, *The Life of John Maynard Keynes* (Penguin 1972) p. 226.

17 Jacques Maritain, *St. Thomas Aquinas*, translated by J. F. Scanlan (Sheed & Ward 1938) pp. 93-4:

> The mind allows itself to be deceived by the mirage of the mythical conception of human nature, which attributes to that nature conditions peculiar to pure spirit, assumes that nature to be in each of us as the angelic nature in the angel.

18 St Thomas Aquinas, *Summa Theologica,* quae. 85, art. 3.

19 Milton Friedman, 'The Role of Monetary Policy', in *The Optimum Quantity of Money and Other Essays* (Aldine Publishing House 1969) p. 109.

20 Herbert Stein, *The Fiscal Revolution in America.* University of Chicago Press 1969.

21 James M. Buchanan and Richard E. Wagner, *Democracy in Deficit, The Political Legacy of Lord Keynes* (Academic Press 1977) p. 96.

22 Buchanan and Wagner, op. cit., p. 102.

8

Complaining about Education Cuts: Materialist Diversions from Proper Concerns

Caroline Cox and John Marks

> There are more things in heaven and earth, Horatio,
> Than are dreamt of in your philosophy.

Consider this statement concerning education:

> Expenditure is to be reduced by 6% a year and although the total number of pupils is expected to fall by 13% nationally this will not allow for current standards to be maintained. Pupil teacher ratios will increase; the range of subjects offered will be reduced; books, materials and equipment will become even scarcer . . . The most recent reports of the School's Inspectors . . . point out that we cannot expect to maintain standards in such an economic climate . . . Not only is expenditure being reduced, the distribution of available resources has been altered, with private schools benefiting at the expense of state schools . . . What is very certain is that the allocation of resources is not being made on established criteria of need but rather in pursuit of a political ideology.

These words come from a document which self-consciously claims to be a Christian statement[1] and which describes itself as 'a deeply caring assessment which grows out of a concern for people'. These few brief sentences encapsulate a style of writing about complex social issues which is, at best, superficial. At worst, it may be positively misleading because it contains so many inaccuracies, misconceptions, unstated assumptions and myths. Let us examine some of these myths.

Myth I
Resources are unlimited

Many writers who claim to care for people often argue as though unlimited resources are available for desirable social purposes. This is clearly untrue since resources, even those available to the government of a modern industrial state, are necessarily finite.

In our view, one mark of true compassion is to realize that priorities need to be balanced and to accept that resources spent, say, on education are not available for health care and vice versa. For example, it can be argued that, as the school population falls in the years ahead, expenditure on education should also fall, at least in relative terms, and thus perhaps release more resources which are badly needed for the health care of the rapidly growing numbers of elderly people, many of whom are frail and infirm.

Myth II
More money means higher standards

Many people in education often state, almost as a reflex response, that this or that educational problem could be solved if more money were made available. The National Union of Teachers is one influential body which tediously asserts this view. Yet such statements confuse the money spent on education — what economists call the inputs to the system — with the standards of attainment or behaviour reached by pupils or students — the outputs of the system. It is an obvious fallacy to confuse outputs with inputs and one which begs the whole question of how best to use scarce resources. And, while some minimum level of expenditure is obviously indispensable to achieve the required output, there is no evidence that more expenditure automatically leads to higher standards of teaching and learning and some evidence that the opposite can be true.[2]

Myth III
Expenditure on education is being cut

This statement is misleading in a number of ways. First, it is misleading because it ignores the dramatic overall *increase* in expenditure on education over the last 30 years — from about 3% to nearly 6% of Gross National Product[3] and by about 300% in real terms. So the resources we choose, and continue to choose, to devote to education are very large indeed.

Secondly, it ignores the fact that expenditure per pupil, in real terms, is higher than ever before in the history of this country. It fails to take into account the rapid fall in the school population due to the fall in birth rate in the 1970s. Just over 700,000 pupils entered secondary schools in September 1982. By 1986 this number will fall to 550,000 and by 1989 to 500,000. Such major demographic changes must surely be taken into account in any responsible assessment of how much ought to be spent on education. And, as mentioned above, these changes may need to be considered with other demographic changes such as the growing numbers of elderly people who will require more, and more expensive, health care in the years ahead.

Myth IV
More teachers automatically mean better education

Since 1950 pupil-teacher ratios have fallen from 30.4 to 23.8 in primary schools, and from 21.1 to 17.0 in secondary schools. There are now fewer children per teacher than there have ever been. But does this mean that standards of attainment or behaviour are higher? Or that these standards have risen in line with the increase in the number of teachers? It would be a brave man who made that claim.

And is there any evidence that further increases in the number of teachers would lead to more teaching and learning? Some recent evidence suggests the opposite.[4] In addition HMIs, in their detailed report on schools in Inner London, were insistent that the provision of teachers and of other resources was generous to a fault but that too often many pupils achieved less than their capabilities. Why? Because many teachers often asked too little of their pupils and because teaching methods, such as mixed ability teaching, leave 'the least able unheeded and the most able unchallenged'.

This evidence supports the commonsense view that it is the quality of teaching that counts and not the quantity of teachers — again a conclusion which ought to be recognized in any responsible and caring commentary on education.

Myth V
In the interests of better education, resources of all kinds should be increased

Statements like this ignore another fundamental economic truth which again is grounded in common sense. In the real world, the resources devoted to education are always finite and the key question is how best to use such inevitably limited resources. Once this truth is recognized, it is but a short step to arrive at the principle of the 'trade-off' and to realize that expenditure on one 'input' to the education system may be rising at the expense of another. This is just what has happened in recent years when the teachers' salary bill has risen dramatically while expenditure on books and equipment has fallen in real terms. Few people realize that if pupil-teacher ratios were to fall to the levels existing only four or five years ago, expenditure on books and equipment could be doubled and on books alone nearly quadrupled. Such obvious considerations ought to be included in any responsible assessment of the resources devoted to education.

By focusing attention on such myths, the kind of attitude and comment quoted at the opening of this chapter deflects the attention of Christians from some of the fundamental educational issues of the day which should be the concern of all who care deeply about the education of the next generation. We propose to redress the balance by considering briefly four of these issues in turn: comprehensive reorganization, religious education in schools, the battle for the curriculum and the future of religious schools.

Comprehensive reorganization

In 1964 fewer than 10% of secondary schoolchildren were in comprehensive schools. Now the figure is more than 90%. This changeover has been called 'one of the most significant developments in secondary education since 1902'[5] and 'an experiment with the life chances of millions of children'.[6] An experiment suggests that we should try to find out what has happened in order to see if the outcome conforms to expectations. Yet this has not been done. The educational researcher Guy Neave surmises that this may be due to the 'political sensitivity' of the issue.

> But does political sensitivity in any way justify failure to monitor the most important reform in secondary education since 1902? The answer must surely be NO. Neither empirically nor morally. Empirically it

remains unjustifiable because without adequate up-to-date information we can only discuss the issue in terms of prejudice . . . Morally unjustifiable also, because, without such enquiries and information, we are, in effect, asking parents to endorse our convictions, beliefs and prejudices either for or against comprehensive education, without the opportunity of making their own judgment on the development of the national system.

> 'Puir wee cow'ring tim'rous beastie
> O what fear's lurking i' thy breastie'[7]

Surely the Churches with their long-standing concern with and involvement in education should have been in the vanguard of those calling for such evaluation and insisting that successive governments met the minimum requirements of public accountability. Yet all too often the Churches have been silent during the public educational controversies of the last twenty years — more concerned to retain their stake in the voluntary schools than to ensure that vital issues of principle in public policy were properly debated and assessed. It has been left to a few individuals, many of them committed Christians, to question the major directions of public policy[8] and later to initiate and carry through research[9] into the often damaging effects of comprehensive reorganization. The first results are now emerging and increase rather than allay fears about the comprehensive experiment.

Religious education in schools

Two major provisions of the 1944 Education Act — for the school day to start with a religious assembly and for the compulsory inclusion of religious instruction in the curriculum — have, in too many schools, been either diluted or ignored.

Secular or humanist assemblies and agreed syllabuses for 'religious education' which contain little that is recognizably Christian are all too common today. It is worth considering this development in the context of the parliamentary debates on the religious clauses of the 1944 Act. Too few people now realize that this legislation on religious education and worship had a high degree of all party support, and that one major reason for this support was the ideological take-over of education then being practised in Germany under Adolf Hitler's National Socialist party.

In the years since 1944 the Churches have allowed the case for religious education to go largely by default in the maintained schools attended by most of the population. And they have capitulated despite evidence that such religious education is wholly in accordance with the wishes of the vast majority of parents.

The moral vacuum thus left by the Churches in many schools is now being filled in some places by other ideologies. It is possible that some of these ideologies could prove as inimical to true education and as harmful to our future as a nation as was the enforced adoption of the National Socialist ideology in the German schools of the 1930s and early 1940s.

The battle for the curriculum

Most teachers and parents are now well aware that religious education is not the only aspect of the school curriculum that is being challenged in Britain today. Topics such as multi-ethnic and multi-cultural education, political education, peace studies and world studies are all currently vying not only for a place on the curriculum but also increasingly to be taught 'across the curriculum'. Syllabuses for the teaching of history, geography, English and even the sciences are in many places now being revised in ways which are politicized to a degree that would have been inconceivable only a few years ago.[10] This is not the place to discuss this complex topic. Nor would we argue that the Church should necessarily take a leading role in such discussions. But we would like to make one comment on the role of the Churches in the debate on peace studies, political education and nuclear weapons.

It is at least arguable that bodies such as the Churches which aspire to moral leadership should have attempted to supply two elements which were lacking in that debate: an appreciation of the moral arguments for the open liberal democratic societies of the West as compared with the closed Marxist societies of Eastern Europe and the Soviet Union;[11] and a realistic discussion of the fate of religion and the Churches in those Marxist societies.[12]

How better to achieve the first of these aims than by drawing attention to the well-documented evidence for the determined and sustained assaults by the rulers of most Marxist states on religious institutions and by recalling the resilience of those institutions under conditions of the most fearsome harassment. Let us not forget that the citizens of Marxist states can often end up in a prison camp or psychiatric hospital for smuggling *Bibles*.

Religious schools

Perhaps the most fundamental duty of the Churches in education is to ensure the continued existence of religious schools — both within and outside the state system of education. This duty has been enshrined over the centuries. Nowadays its importance is publicly recognized in the general acceptance of the right of independent religious schools to exist and in the arrangements for voluntary denominational schools made under the 1944 Education Act.

The vital importance of religious schools, independent of the state, has recently been publicly restated by Pope John Paul II:

> The individual being educated has the right to choose the system of education and therefore the type of school that he or she prefers. From this it clearly follows that, in principle, a state monopoly of education is not permissible, and that only a pluralism of school systems will respect the fundamental right and freedom of individuals . . . The Church offers the Catholic school as a specific and enriching contribution to this variety of school possibilities.[13]

Perhaps the Pope had the experiences of the Churches in Eastern Europe in mind. We suggest that the Churches in Britain could follow the Pope's example in making clear their principled opposition to any attempt, present or future, to abolish all schools which are independent of the state. Yet, they have been strangely silent about the Labour Party's firm commitment to abolish *all* independent schools.

We also suggest that it might be appropriate for the Churches to be more forthright in their opposition to the cutbacks in the existing voluntary religious denomination schools. There is considerable evidence that these schools are popular with parents — many are oversubscribed at a time of falling school rolls. There is also evidence that many Local Education Authorities are trying to counter this popularity and to prop up their unpopular schools by insisting that *all* schools, popular and unpopular alike, should take their 'fair' share of reduced intakes.[14]

The Churches should resist these pressures in the interests of the children whose parents are practising Christians. And perhaps they should also be willing to reserve some places for other pupils too. Although we recognize that there may be a 'critical mass' beyond which any increase could affect the ethos of the school, there is much to be said for encouraging some children to be educated in an atmosphere of Christian beliefs and values — even if their parents are not churchgoers but choose a church school for their children.

It could be argued that the secular intellectual and moral trends arising during the Enlightenment need to be complemented with a spiritual dimension and that this is one way in which the Churches could make a valuable contribution to the life of the nation wholly in character with their historic mission.

Conclusion

We do not have the arrogance to believe that the fundamental questions we have posed and the answers we have indicated are in any sense final. In the complex real world, social, political and theological questions are seldom susceptible of complete or final answers. What we do believe is that some of the issues we have raised are of fundamental importance and that the contribution of the Churches to these debates often leaves much to be desired. It is our hope that they will scrupulously desist from confused and ill-informed politicizing and that instead they will conscientiously offer the spiritual leadership for which they are uniquely suited. This leadership is urgently needed because, in the words of the hymn:

> New occasions teach new duties;
>   Time makes ancient good uncouth;
> They must upward still and onward
>   Who would keep abreast of truth.

H. W. Longfellow, A Psalm of Life

NOTES

1 *The Cuts and the Wounds — A Christian response to cuts in public spending,* Internal Economy Group, Thames North Province Church and Society Panel, 1982.

2 HMI, *Educational Provision by the Inner London Education Authority,* Department of Education and Science, 1980; 'When Big Spending Equals Low Grades', *Times Educational Supplement,* 10 Oct. 1982; J. Marks, C. Cox and M. Pomian-Srzednicki, *Standards in English Schools — An analysis of the examination results of secondary schools in England for 1981,* National Council for Educational Standards, 1983.

3 Compare the proportion spent on defence: in 1960 the ratio of defence to education spending was 1.75 but by 1974 education had overtaken defence and the ratio had fallen to 0.87.

4 See J. Marks *et al.* in note 2 above.

5 G. Neave, 'Sense and Sensitivity: The Case of Comprehensive Education', in *Quantitative Sociology Newsletter* 21, 1979.

6 By the socialist sociologist Julienne Ford, in *Social Class and the Comprehensive School* (Routledge & Kegan Paul 1969).

7 G. Neave, op. cit.

8 For example in the well-known Black Papers on Education, edited by Professor C. B. Cox, A. E. Dyson and Dr Rhodes Boyson.

9 R. W. Baldwin, *Secondary Schools 1965-1979,* National Council for Educational Standards (1981); J. Marks *et al.,* note 2 above.

10 Whereas politicization in the classroom is always dubious, it is even more disturbing if it is biased and propagandist. Most of these developments are instigated and implemented by left-wing Local Education Authorities and teachers.

11 See C. Cox and J. Marks, 'What has Athens to do with Jerusalem?', in C. Cox and J. Marks, ed., *The Right to Learn — Purpose, Professionalism and Accountability in State Education,* Centre for Policy Studies, 1982.

12 T. Beeson, *Discretion and Valour* (Collins/Fontana 1975); M. Pomian-Srzednicki and A. Tomský, 'Marxism: The Compulsion to Neighbourly Love', this volume, pp. 116-22.

13 *Lay Catholics in Schools: Witnesses to Faith,* Incorporated Catholic Truth Society, 1982.

14 C. Cox and J. Marks, 'Parents' Freedom Threatened — Attack on Church Schools', *The Free Nation,* July 1982; Rev. Dr J. Gay, *The Debate about Church Schools in the Oxford Diocese,* Culham College Institute, 1982.

9

The Folly of Politicized Welfare

Ralph Harris

Goodies versus baddies?

As a stumbling member of the Church of England, I certainly feel in need of the special ministrations that bishops should be well placed to offer in teaching a firmer faith in God, more active repentance of sins and more extensive reform of our relations with less lovely neighbours. Yet one of the most disillusioning experiences since joining the crossbenchers in the House of Lords has been to find many bishops mostly talking much the same secular stuff that comes more naturally from the dwindling Labour benches. Thus I do not recall a speech from either source urging restraint in any aspect of swollen government spending, or acknowledging the remotest possibility of excess or abuse in social policy.

I hope some of my new-found friends on the Labour benches would rise above politics sufficiently to refrain from claiming that endorsement by bishops proves their economic and social theories are necessarily better than mine, much less ordained by God. Indeed, any fruitful dialogue on the future of the welfare state must start from acknowledging that equally good men can adopt sharply contrasting views even on such widely-accepted institutions as the National Health Service, free school and university education, subsidized council housing, and universal, compulsory state 'insurance' for retirement pensions and other social benefits.

My modest aim here is not to outline a comprehensive alternative to these increasingly failing policies.[1] It is simply to argue that there is a powerful economic, moral and political critique which has brought academics to contemplate a more selective approach and which should open more Christian minds and hearts to the desirability of radical reform. In other words, my plea is to get away from discussing the welfare state as a battleground between 'goodies' who always want to spend more on it and 'baddies' who believe there are better ways to help those who cannot help themselves. I can imagine that some opponents of the welfare state don't give a damn for the poor. Even more am I certain that many on both sides in politics who boast shamelessly of their 'compassion' are chiefly after feeling good or buying votes — at other people's expense.

Free lunch for (almost) all?

If I had to take a single text to illuminate the gross error that passes for argument in favour of more spending on welfare it would be from a bishop, whose name I prefer not to advertise,[2] in a Lords debate on alleged 'cuts' in welfare spending. To prove the 'inevitability' of increasing dependency on government aid 'for all citizens' our mercifully anonymous bishop offered the following self-evident nonsense:

> The image of strong, independent citizens who do not need help from the resources of others is feasible for only *a very few* privileged people. (italics added)

In case their Lordships were hard of hearing, our bishop hammered home his rubber nail:

> Today, the *great majority of people* — and I include myself — depend upon the social wage to maintain the quality of life.

Here is the economic fallacy of the 'free lunch'. Is it entirely forgivable, even for an unworldly bishop, to preach the falsehood that the welfare state enables (almost) everyone to live better at the expense of somebody else? Plainly, if community support were concentrated on the declining minority in need, as I would prefer, the modest cost could be borne by 'others', namely the better-off. But as comprehensive welfare services have come to be extended to all comers, the mounting cost must fall on ever-widening sections of the population. Thus in Britain the total bill for state education, medical care, housing and social security exceeded £64 billion in 1981, which was more than half of all government spending and approaching 30% of the total national income. How can anyone believe that such massive sums could be raised chiefly from 'a very few privileged people'?

The reality is, of course, quite otherwise. To finance universal welfare benefits, on top of all other government services, politicians have pushed income tax (including 'national insurance' contributions) up to a marginal rate of 39% on incomes as low as one-third of average earnings. At the same time, VAT and other 'regressive' taxes on spending by rich and poor alike have been raised to produce a higher total than the yield from the 'progressive' tax on incomes. If we compare the taxes paid by families of varying size and income with the value of the social benefits they respectively derive from the various state services, we discover the truth trumpeted by many IEA publications that most families more than pay their own way in welfare.

This simple reality was vividly exposed by former Labour MP Brian Walden, in a trenchant attack on 'The six evils sown by Lloyd George' with his vote-buying offer of 'ninepence for fourpence' in 1911.[3] Mr Walden concluded his discussion of the third evil as follows:

> It has ceased to be a case of robbing Peter to pay Paul. The current reality is the extraction from poor Paul's pocket of rather more than is subsequently shoved back inside his shirt.

So far from being chiefly concerned with bringing support to people in need, the complex apparatus of the welfare state has been described by Mr Arthur Seldon[4] as largely engaged in carrying financial coals back and forth to Newcastle, with heavy freight charges in both directions.

As an old politician, Mr Walden shrewdly referred to:

> The Byzantine complexity of the arrangements needed to maintain the pretence that a genuine transfer of wealth from society in general to the majority of individuals in particular is actually taking place.

Taxed into poverty?

While this tax-benefit mangle is not, therefore, principally a method of redistributing existing income from the better-off to the worse-off, it certainly has a major effect in reducing total incomes. Although economists can argue endlessly about the initial 'impact' of taxes and their eventual 'incidence', few would doubt that all taxes above a moderate level have depressing and distorting effects on work and investment. If higher earnings are severely taxed, most victims are likely to prefer more leisure to engage in do-it-yourself activities, or be more tempted into the black market. If successful entrepreneurs are singled out for savage taxation, they are more likely to seek the comfort of off-shore havens where their money and talents may yield nothing to the grasping Inland Revenue. On a more prosaic level, as higher taxes, 'national insurance' and rates have burdened British costs of production, sales at home and abroad are handicapped against foreign competition, with obvious damage to domestic employment.

These and other ill effects of high taxation may be less obvious to bishops who lack training in economic analysis and whose 'business' enjoys some tax exemption and rate abatement under the heading of a religious charity. But they can hardly be excused ignorance of the evil consequences for individual and family responsibility of a tax-welfare system that tempts millions to prefer dependency in subsidized idleness to self-support in paid employment. This well-known general dilemma was recently particularized in horrifying detail by a foremost authority, Hermione Parker, in the *Moral Hazards of Social Benefits*.[5] Among the dozens of case studies documented by Mrs Parker, a middling example is that a married man with wife and two small children would require weekly earnings above £130 to be £10 better-off working than living on supplementary benefits. After extensive review of the evidence, Mrs Parker concludes that around five million adults risk being trapped in poverty or unemployment by the perversion of incentives that render social benefits more attractive than making the effort to support themselves and their families. Many who could earn below-average incomes are thus in plain truth taxed into poverty and voluntary unemployment. The majority who do earn average or higher incomes are taxed into dependence on 'free' welfare services. That leaves only a minority of rich or self-sacrificing parents who, having been taxed for state education or medicine they don't like, can afford to pay twice for choice of private schools or medical insurance.

Motives v. morals?

Since the Elizabethan Poor Law of 1601, governments have rightly come to accept the duty of providing a minimum income below which no citizen shall fall. But is it truly 'compassionate' to allow the safety net to become a hammock that corrupts the will to work? It is no use for proponents of ever more expensive welfare arrangements to profess their good intentions, least of all when the cost is imposed on others including the supposed beneficiaries. The seminal insight of Adam Smith and other pioneers of market analysis was that good intentions which fly in the face of incentives risk quite opposite results.

The general motive of the market is that most people, most of the time, will best exert their God-given energies and talents if there is some relationship between effort and anticipated reward *in some form*. It simply will not do for Christians or apparently high-minded humanists to denounce what Adam Smith upheld as 'the effort of every man to better his condition' as unworthy materialism or naked self-interest. Although nicely calculated to evoke admiration and applause such lofty rhetoric often amounts to little more than pandering for popularity by a condescending, even contemptuous, attack on ordinary people. It is like currying the favour of overweight diners-out by blaming the waiter for their obesity.

In his profoundly confused and contradictory testament *Bias to the Poor*, the Bishop of Liverpool rightly wishes 'to reach down to the deepest springs which motivate people'. He talks of 'the heart and soul finding fulfilment in doing worthwhile work' in return for 'a modest personal income'. Yet he settles for having it both ways by refraining from condemning the wage-grab excesses of the trade union monopoly that helped destroy the London and Liverpool docks, and elsewhere[6] he wins easy, unreflecting popularity by complaining:

> The voluntary bodies used to pay a pittance. They imposed on a worker's sense of vocation. Perhaps the Church has done the same thing in its years.

But how can a Christian or anyone else show a 'sense of vocation' or 'fulfilment in worthwhile work' except by offering his services for less than they could command elsewhere? Are we no longer permitted to look forward to reaping part of our reward for sacrifice in heaven?

The trouble with such confused critics is that they are so frightened by their own phantoms of 'economic man' that they miss the true glory of the market place — of which bishops, voluntary organizations, Church Commissioners, are all part.[7] Thus none of us is compelled to seek out the highest monetary reward for our efforts. The beauty of a free society is that all of us can choose what combination of material benefits and other satisfactions we will maximize in return for our services or spending. The real motive for high endeavour of all kinds is not narrow, pecuniary self-interest but a wide range of *self-chosen purposes*. Nor is there any contradiction in people freely rendering services to their chosen causes like the Church, the local community, poorer members of their family or less fortunate neighbours, whilst driving as hard a bargain as they can with any employer who can afford to pay a higher wage without damaging future employment. After all, in a competitive market (not dominated by unbridled union power) high wages and prices indicate the most economic use of scarce human and material sources.

It is no doubt a grievous commentary on fallen man that we do not display in our everyday conduct a higher concern than we commonly do for the welfare of others. But surely it is a large part of the Christian purpose to widen our sympathies, raise our sights and purify the mixed motives on which we act — in the Church or family, no less than in the market. If the Church had been more successful in elevating human nature, the market in which people work, spend, save and invest would reflect those higher standards of behaviour, the absence of which the more politicized bishops constantly lament and conveniently blame on 'the market'! Yet their secular gospel of socialism strains after an approach to heaven-on-earth that would make far higher demands on unselfish sharing and self-sacrifice. The dilemma they dodge is that, in the absence of a transformation of human nature, sharing and sacrifice would have to be ruthlessly imposed by state power that must rob such qualities of any vestige of virtue. Not only does the resulting spread of coercion do violence to free choice, which is a condition of moral conduct, it also deadens the mainspring of efficient production, which is a condition of continuing to improve the lot of the poorest. At the beginning of the century, the first (and certainly the noblest) Cambridge Professor of economics, Alfred Marshall, wrote the following warning to his fellow social reformers:

The world under free enterprise will fall far short of the finest ideals until economic chivalry is developed. But until it is developed, every step in the direction of collectivism is a grave menace to the maintenance even of our present moderate rate of progress.[8]

Corruption of democracy

The crowning paradox of well-meaning Christian socialists from Archbishop Temple to Bishop Sheppard, is that their secular remedy for fallible human nature makes no allowance for human nature in politics. The Labour Party makes larger claims than Conservatives or Liberals to an explicit Christian inspiration.[9] Yet its bid for support is always pitched in terms of the voter's self-interest rather than appealing to voluntary sacrifice. Thus in 1983 Labour's manifesto amounted to little more than a shopping list of free benefits for pensioners, unemployed, families, children, and every kind of minority pressure group with grievances, true or imagined. Under 'A New Deal for Pensioners' there were no fewer than twelve promises of higher income in cash and kind with not a single word on the cost or source of finance. When a growing majority of people can expect to retire with a second pension drawn from their work and a home free from mortgage, it is obvious that such indiscriminate political largess is not chiefly motivated by a wish to help people who are unable to help themselves. Since pensioners form approaching one quarter of the electorate, this naked bid for votes is simply a more blatant example of the corruption of 'welfare' without regard to need which we see elsewhere in council house subsidies, rent control, child benefits, maternity grants, death grants; 'new deals' for widows, working women, single parent families, and, of course, improved 'free' health care, education and personal social services.

It is no use Bishop Sheppard[10] pretending that all or most of these bribes are 'rights' conferred by 'national insurance', which no longer bears any relation to the prudent principles of funding contributions. Their 'pay as you go' financing is indistinguishable from general taxation, which we have seen operates to reduce most incomes to the point where all but a minority are made dependent on state welfare. Nor does the corruption of politics stop there. Because benefits are more electorally 'profitable' than the taxes necessary to finance them, politicians of all parties, and in most countries,[11] have been driven to chronic over-spending. To this sin we can trace the source of inflation, with all its evil consequences for the economy, polity and society. By the fraudulent process of robbing savings of their value, the resulting debasement of money by irresponsible politicians strikes at the very thrift which is the foundation of individual independence, family security and national stability.

In a notable maiden speech in the House of Lords,[12] the outstanding international economist Lord (Peter) Bauer proclaimed that the 'fundamental issue' of the welfare state was moral rather than economic, not least because it spreads dependency by reducing adults to the status of children who are left with pocket money rather than being trusted with responsibility for managing their own incomes. But even if the moral and political consequences were less deplorable, the economic results must ultimately prove unendurable. There should be no surprise that as more money has been devoted to 'free' welfare, complaints have multiplied about lack of nursery schools, low standards in secondary schools, queues in doctors' surgeries, lengthening waiting lists for hospital beds and lack of houses to rent. Since pricing is the only way demand and supply can be brought into harmony without some form of rationing, it should not require a higher degree in economics to predict that 'free' (or heavily subsidized) services will be over-demanded and under-supplied.

It is not only the articulate middle classes (including Labour MPs) who will deploy social push and political pull to get their children to the better schools (and on to university), or to jump the queue for the best the NHS can offer. As real incomes continue to rise, an increasing majority of working people will want their families to enjoy the higher standards in education and medical care[13] that they have come to take for granted in their homes, holidays and hobbies. But so long as politicians try to monopolize such welfare services — for their own electoral purposes — governments will find increasing difficulty in raising the finance for improvements through ever more oppressive taxation. The case for encouraging direct payment in place of taxation was bluntly expressed by the senior Labour politician, Douglas (now Lord) Houghton:

While people would be willing to pay for better services for themselves, they may not be willing to pay more in taxes as a kind of insurance premium which may bear no relation to the services actually received.[14]

The politicization of welfare can thus be shown to suffer from a multitude of defects, difficulties and dangers, inseparable from trying to finance 'free' services for everyone through the over-worked mechanism of taxation and inflation. The outlook is further darkened by recent experience of the so-called 'public service' trade unions which have learned to batten on state schools and the NHS as though they were run for the comfort of teachers and hospital employees rather than for the benefit of children and patients. The result can only be to intensify the difficulty of controlling costs and improving efficiency in state monopoly welfare services.

Is it not time we heeded the wisdom of the great classical economic philosophers of the last century who saw government welfare policy as a passing phase towards the fullest flowering of individual freedom and fulfilment? From a rich literature of elevated social speculation and analysis, I commend two samples. The first is from John Stuart Mill in 1848:

> The mode in which government can most surely demonstrate the sincerity by which it intends the greatest good of its subjects is by doing the things which are made incumbent upon it by the helplessness of the public, in such a manner as shall tend not to increase and perpetuate but to correct that helplessness . . . government aid . . . should be so given as to be as far as possible a course of education for the people in the art of accomplishing great objects by individual energy and voluntary co-operation.

The second from Nassau Senior in 1861 was a vision of the future which could now be ours to secure and cherish:

> We may look forward to the time when the labouring population may be safely entrusted with the education of their children; . . . the assistance and superintendence . . . of the Government for that purpose . . . [is] . . . only a means of preparing the labouring classes for a better, but remote state of things . . . in the latter part of the twentieth century . . . when that assistance and superintendence shall no longer be necessary.

After more than a century of growing up, might the 1980s mark our coming of age?

NOTES

1 A long reading list could be drawn from the publications of the IEA, starting perhaps with *Over-ruled on Welfare*, Hobart Paperback 13, published in 1979.

2 But so as not to conceal my source, I give the reference to the *Lords Hansard* for 8 April 1981, col. 561.

3 *The Standard*, 28 June 1983.

4 Arthur Seldon, *Charge*. Temple Smith 1977.

5 Hermione Parker, *The Moral Hazards of Social Benefits*, Research Monograph 37, IEA, 1982.

6 *Lord's Hansard*, loc. cit., col. 546.

7 In *Bias to the Poor* (Hodder & Stoughton 1983) Bishop Sheppard complains that 'the emphasis on efficiency in the free market' closes down businesses 'in areas from which the market has shifted away' (p. 136), yet later he defends the 'painful process of making some churches redundant in areas where the population has drastically reduced' (p. 219).

8 Alfred Marshall, 'Social Possibilities of Economic Chivalry', *Economic Journal*, March 1967.

9 In a rousing speech before the 1983 election, Mr Roy Hattersley called for 'a crusade' of the 'most passionate evangelism', which included 'spreading the word' and 'preaching the gospel to the faithful' so as to 'rout the unbelievers'.

10 Sheppard, op. cit., p. 177.

11 *The World Crisis in Social Security*, ed. Jean-Jacques Rosa for the Institute of Contemporary Studies, San Francisco 1982.

12 *Lord's Hansard*, 29 June 1983, cols. 274-5.

13 A survey conducted for BUPA by NOP found that trade union members in their national sample voted 3 to 1 against the statement that 'Companies should *not* be allowed to offer their workers job benefits like private medical treatment'.

14 Douglas Houghton, *Paying for the Social Services*, Occasional Paper 16, IEA, 1967.

PART II

Fundamental Issues

10

*Christianity and Capitalism**

Brian Griffiths

The basic ethos of capitalism is definitely anti-Christian: it is the maximizing of economic gain, the raising of man's grasping impulse, the idolizing of the strong, the subordination of man to economic production. Humanization is for capitalism an unintended by-product . . . solidarity is for capitalism accidental.[1]

The market is the institutionalisation of individualism and non-responsibility. Neither buyer nor seller is responsible for anything but himself.[2]

The Christian Church has never found it easy to come to terms with the market place. Since the early Church's first short-lived experiment with communism, there have been Christians for whom private property, interest and profit are at best dubious and at worst immoral. Statements by contemporary Christians, such as those above, suggest that a more virulent and widespread antagonism towards the market economy has developed within the Church during the last quarter of a century. The dependence of the market economic system on the profit motive, individualistic self-interest and the competitive spirit render it morally indefensible in the eyes of its critics. And the materialistic and unequal society it seems to foster is judged to be utterly at variance with the teachings of Jesus on wealth, poverty and community.[3]

Free markets versus poverty

But the problem of capitalism's legitimacy is more complex than this rhetoric implies. As a matter of historical fact, the market economy has been responsible for the transformation of the Western world from widespread poverty and degradation to an

---

*This chapter summarizes arguments from the author's *The Creation of Wealth*, forthcoming from Hodder & Stoughton 1984.

unprecedented spreading of prosperity. Similarly in the contemporary world, the market economies of the West have been able to create wealth more efficiently and have secured for the poorest of their people a far higher level of per capita consumption than have the state-owned and state-planned economies of the socialist block. In the Third World today, the remarkable success of market-oriented economies such as Taiwan, South Korea, Singapore in East Asia, and to a lesser but significant extent the Ivory Coast, Kenya and Malawi in Africa, in harnessing the inventiveness and entrepreneurial resources of their peoples is in marked contrast to the disappointing economic performance of countries that have relied on state-planning and regulation, such as India, Tanzania and Mozambique. Three crucially important factors that have enabled market economies to generate wealth more effectively than state-dominated ones are their greater reliance on private rather than state enterprise as the driving force of economic development, the larger scope given to choice in free markets, and their active encouragement of international trade and foreign investment. It is these which have produced relative success.

Taken on its own, this economic superiority would be of little significance if the raising of living standards were not such a matter of concern to political leaders and churchmen alike — a concern echoed in the ceaseless demands for more redistribution of wealth in favour of the poor both on a national and global scale. The case for an anti-poverty policy is certainly a strong one since higher rates of economic growth cannot by themselves be relied upon to achieve a reduction in absolute poverty. However the redistribution of wealth alone will not solve the world's economic problem. Indeed, by breeding dependence on handouts, the redistribution of wealth through the coercive power of the state can make matters worse.

For Christians concerned about poverty, the relationship between capitalism and development in the case of Taiwan is particularly instructive. Here is a Third World country with a rapidly growing economy that has experienced a reduction in levels of absolute poverty and a greater equality of income distribution. Growth with equity has been achieved through policies that provided for an initial redistribution of assets by land reform, the privatization of public enterprises in the early stages of the country's growth, the removal of protectionist controls on commodity and labour prices, the pursuit of export-oriented rather than import-substitution policies together with an open-door policy to foreign investment, and a policy of decentralization that has encouraged the development of small-scale industry in rural areas.[4]

Conflict with Christian principles?

Similar examples demonstrate that there is a strong *economic* case to be made for the market economy as the most efficient system for the creation of wealth. There is furthermore ample evidence to refute the claim that the market economy is necessarily hostile to equitable development.[5] But this is only one, and perhaps for many Christians, the least important dimension of the problem of the legitimacy of capitalism. Much more difficult is the apparent inconsistency between the teachings of Jesus and the apostles and the very principles on which the market economy depends for success.

Contrary to the claims of some contemporary theologians, it is not possible to deduce socialism from Jesus' teaching about the Kingdom of God. Neither is it possible to regard the market economy as a logical outgrowth of that Kingdom. The messianic claims of Jesus and his proclamation of the Kingdom of God were never intended to be understood in political terms. Much as some modern Christians would have liked him to, Jesus did not address himself directly to practical questions concerning the creation of wealth or the removal of poverty, and it is significant that he chose not to do so. Because the Kingdom of God depends for its very existence on an inward supernatural power, it is impossible to translate it into contemporary social, political and economic institutions. An attempt to legislate the ideals of the Kingdom of God into practice immediately comes up against the fact that the real world is made up of fallen human beings and is not a community of saints. To cope with this reality, we need stronger social and economic disciplines than those that would be appropriate for a community radically and inwardly transformed by the presence of the Holy Spirit. Insofar as the Judeao-Christian religion deals with principles for ordering socio-economic life in a fallen world, it is to the laws of the Pentateuch rather than the spontaneous sharing of the early Church that we should look. Above all, the Old Testament background is fundamental to an understanding of Jesus' teaching on economic matters.

The Old Testament view

Central to the Hebrew view of the material world is the belief that it is created by God and that it is intrinsically good. There is in creation an abundance and bounty, the promise of a land flowing with milk and honey. Poverty, famine and misery are not part of the Creator's intention for the world. Man, created in the image of God, has been delegated authority to subdue and rule the physical world. Indeed, the urge to harness and control the resources of nature is part of what it means to be made in God's image. This 'creation mandate' is not however an excuse for provoking an ecological crisis, since man is accountable to God as a trustee for the preservation and care of the material world.

This distinctive biblical view of the material world and of man's task within it has major implications for economic life. It gives complete legitimacy to what an economist would refer to as a responsible form of wealth creation — the transformation of the material world so that it is of more use to fellow human beings. A businessman concerned with construction, manufacturing, agriculture, extraction or services is therefore involved in the complex task of fulfilling this 'creation mandate'. But to allow the legitimacy of wealth creation is not to endow it with autonomy — to do so would be to justify a philosophy of materialism. The world God created is also spiritual and the call to seek first the Kingdom of God enjoins us to live by the laws of his Kingdom within the material world. The challenge for the Christian then is not to reject the material world and the business of wealth creation in favour of some higher spiritual priority, but to serve others through the process of wealth creation in the process of serving God.

As regards property rights, there is never any suggestion in the Pentateuch that the state or community should be accorded rights of ownership over the land. For Christians who believe some form of common ownership is more just or equitable than private property rights, the pattern of land distribution that followed the Israelites' entry to the Promised Land is hard to explain. If ever there were a situation that might have called for a policy of collective ownership — similar perhaps to Nyerere's Ujaama policy in Tanzania — it was then. Yet each family received a parcel of land to which absolute rights of ownership were attached. Far from violating the principle of God's ultimate ownership of land and man's responsibility as trustee, the granting of inviolable property rights to individual families was essential to its maintenance. If the land were communally owned and controlled by the priests, for example, the whole concept of trusteeship (in the sense of each person being responsible before God for his use of the resources entrusted to him) would have been redundant.

It is also true, however, that constraints were built into the Mosaic law to put a sharp brake on the accumulation of property in a few hands. The Jubilee laws, with their provision for the cancellation of debt, the release of slaves and the return of property to its original owner every fiftieth year, were designed to prevent the development of a cycle of permanent deprivation. And behind this principle of periodic restoration of an equitable distribution of wealth was the idea that the people were the tenants of Yahweh.

In their outspoken criticism of the social and economic injustices of ancient Israelite society, the Old Testament prophets have proved a potent source of inspiration for many contemporary Christian critics of capitalism. However, although the prophets exposed the social malaise of their societies, the attack on injustice was never conducted in purely socio-economic terms. The prophets indicted the rich for exploiting the poor, yet they never suggested that the remedy was therefore a redistribution of wealth undertaken in some sort of religious vacuum. They invariably pinpointed the root cause of the trouble as spiritual and in this they showed great insight. Economic injustice was one consequence of the nation's departure from God. Without a simultaneous commitment to changed values and behaviour (which is what repentance means), socio-economic reform by means of the legal and coercive powers of the state would be of no avail.

From those Old Testament attitudes to the material world, property and justice — assumed by Jesus in all his teaching — a number of principles emerge. Private property rather than social ownership of wealth and the means of production is the norm. Permanent access by each family to a stake in economic life is guaranteed. And some form of anti-poverty programme is written into the laws to ensure just and compassionate treatment for the economically weak. In all this there is nothing to suggest that the basic institutions of Western market economies are incompatible with a Christian world view. Indeed these biblical principles seem more compatible with the modern concept of a social market economy than with some variant of Marxism.

False assumptions

Let us now turn to the major ethical objections to the market economy. The condemnation of capitalism as a system founded on greed and self-interest involves three false assumptions. Firstly, it implies that we can live in two worlds — a world of the market place in which the profit motive reduces all behaviour to the low pursuit of self-interest, and the world of the family, local community, and voluntary service in which caring attitudes and a spirit of service prevail. Such a division would be impossible to justify either logically or empirically. It is not the environment that determines the morality of behaviour but the individuals making the decisions. Selfish aggressive individuals can be found in families, schools, hospitals and public service as well as in business. Similarly a businessman committed to certain moral principles can actively seek the welfare of his staff and clients in the context of his commercial activities.

Secondly, it is assumed that the profit motive which dominates the market economy is necessarily a corrupting influence. However, profit-seeking is not confined to the business community and is not judged in the same severe fashion when it appears in other contexts. A trade unionist seeking the best deal for his members or the housewife shopping for the best bargain is acting no differently in principle from a business executive trying to cut costs in the interests of customers, markets and share-holders. Nor is the church committee which seeks competitive tenders for the repair of the fabric. It is furthermore impossible to make a logical connection between profits and single-minded subservience to the profit motive. The fact that businesses have to operate within a budget (as do families, charities and

110

governments) does not mean that financial considerations *alone* determine business behaviour: one cannot move automatically from an accounting concept to a psychological theory.

Finally, self-interest is not synonymous with selfishness. As the dominical command to love our neighbour as ourselves confirms, it can be characteristic of the highest as well as the lowest forms of human behaviour. Self-interest is not a consequence of the fall, although its distortion as selfishness is. The Christian should accept that self-interest as well as selfishness are hallmarks of the world in which we live. There is no point therefore in designing economic systems based on an unrealistic view of man and expecting governments to manipulate that system for the common good. In this light, the Christian might acknowledge the wisdom of Adam Smith, who faced up to the challenge of how to use both legitimate self-interest and selfishness in the interests of the wider community.

Competition versus co-operation

Another major criticism of the market economy is that the competition on which it depends for success is in direct conflict with the Christian ideal of co-operation, with the implication that collectivism in one form or another is morally superior to competitive markets. In thinking about competition it is important to define it in as neutral a way as possible, by saying that it is essentially a way of resolving conflicts of interest and judgement that result from trying to make the best use of scarce resources. Indeed if one analyses the Latin root of the word, one could define competition as the act of striving together with others in pursuit of the best solution to a problem. In economics, competition is to be distinguished sharply both from low rivalry and criminal behaviour. It is, moreover, a means to an end and not an end in itself. In judging the ethics of competition therefore we have to compare them with the ethics of alternative systems, such as the allocation of resources according to political criteria. However, all this avoids the basic question of whether competition can be regarded as a Christian ideal. Clearly, if one examines the teaching and experience of the early Church, competition is not something to which the Church, as the Body of Christ, aspires explicitly, though certainly the disciples competed in service of their Master. However in a world far removed from the Christian ideal and in which scarcity is still a fundamental problem, there is a case for competitive markets as a superior method of allocating resources to benefit the greatest number of ordinary people.

Another moral objection to the market economy is that it produces inequality. For the Christian, the starting point in relating inequality to biblical concepts of justice is the recognition of the basic differences which exist in creation and which are thrown into even greater contrast by the fall, and of the sanctity attached to individual property rights in the Mosaic law. Within this framework, there is no problem in defending the morality of economic inequalities that result from differences in skills, energy, ambition and the freedom to work, innovate, invest and trade. Whilst we cannot justify *every* kind of inequality thrown up by a market economy, within a fallen world inequality of income is an essential aspect of Christian justice. Of course as Hayek and others specifically acknowledge, differences in income do not correspond to differences in intrinsic moral worth. For the Christian who sees his work as a vocation, its moral worth in the sight of God is unrelated to the economic value attached to it in the market place. The challenge for the Christian is this: a certain degree of inequality is necessary in society if human dignity and freedom are to be preserved and if basic standards of justice are to be achieved (it is important that people receive a just reward for their work). But at the same time, wealth involves responsibility and the Christian as a steward is called to share his resources voluntarily with others. From this perspective, the libertarian defence of inequality is unacceptable in that it emphasizes property rights to the exclusion of any responsibility to others, particularly the economically weak members of society; but egalitarianism is also one-sided in that it emphasizes responsibilities to the exclusion of rights. The Christian perspective is unique in that it emphasizes both rights and responsibilities. The more we can *persuade* people to act in this spirit, the closer economic behaviour will coincide with our Christian ideals. But free choice is essential for moral conduct.

Individualism

The last major criticism of the market economy is that it

presupposes a philosophy and spirit of individualism, or worse still of 'possessive individualism'. This is a very important objection to the market economy and care is needed in tracing its theological and philosophical roots. The foundations of modern individualism go back to Stoic philosophy and political individualism, from which it is but a short step to economic individualism and capitalism. The origins of this kind of individualism are profoundly anti-Christian in that rational self-development is seen as the purpose of life. Man is accorded final sovereignty over himself, his capacities and his property, and the community is regarded as an association of freely consenting adults joined together in pursuit of self-determined goals. Yet while this form of individualism is alien to a Christian understanding of man, individuality is part of creation itself and certain of the insights of individualism are valuable. The rival doctrine of man that sees society as dominated by class and group interests and the individual as no more than a tool of the collective, is simply a deficient view of what it means to be human.

The case for the market

So far we have considered the moral objections to the market economy; now it is time to put forward the positive side. The basic argument for a market economy is that for all its imperfections, it is a system that pays respect to human dignity because it allows human freedom. It permits individuals the freedom to buy and sell, save and invest, choose their preferred form of employment and develop the skills they feel appropriate. It allows minorities the same rights too. Socialism does not: it pays scant respect to human dignity because it denies human freedom and forever restricts economic choices. Both systems have been put to the test and we can examine the record, comparing fact with fact and ideal with ideal. If we look at the facts we observe that in one country after another the attempt to create a socialist utopia with property rights vested in the state, has led to the direction of investment and labour, a loss of personal freedom and the growth of the totalitarian state.[6]

The final dimension to the relation between capitalism and

113

Christianity is ideological. Capitalism can be thought of as a historical phenomenon or as an economic system, but it also encompasses ideological elements. Over the past two hundred years, there have been many outstanding attempts to defend the capitalist system. What is interesting is that each of them has been firmly grounded in the prevailing philosophical outlook of its time and none of them can be considered independently of ideology. Whether we look at Adam Smith in the eighteenth century, Herbert Spencer in the nineteenth century, or Friedman and Hayek in our own, all the major intellectual defences of capitalism as an economic system have been conducted within the context of a thoroughly secular philosophy, which is a direct product of the Enlightenment. The common feature is that they all attempt to present economic life as something which is impersonal, amoral, which can be expressed as a 'system' and which, as a system, has a natural tendency to equilibrium. God is pushed into the background and economic life becomes independent of anything divine or indeed, ultimately, anything human as well.

It is difficult on Christian grounds to accept the ideological underpinnings of these defences of capitalism. Firstly, economic life has to be judged within a moral framework — efficiency is not enough. Secondly, it is important to think about economics as actions of individual people not systems. The belief in the system's tendency towards equilibrium emphasizes the economic machine to the exclusion of people. It is imperative therefore from a Christian point of view to rescue the market economy from its narrow secular ideology. From an economic, theological and moral point of view there is much that is of value in the market economy: for the Christian the challenge is to incorporate those aspects within a framework that is distinctively Christian and subject to Christian values.

NOTES

1   Jose Miguez Bonino, *Christians and Marxists: the Mutual Challenge to Revolution* (Hodder & Stoughton 1976) p. 114.

2   E. F. Schumacher, *Small is Beautiful* (Abacus Books 1973) p. 36.

3   See sections 5 and 6 of Rachel Steare's bibliographical chapter in this volume for a selection of Christian critiques of the market economy.

4   For a detailed study of the Taiwan success story, see John C. H. Fei, Gustav Ranis, Shirley W. Y. Kuo, *Growth with Equity: The Taiwan Case* (Oxford University Press for the World Bank 1979).

5   Gary S. Fields, *Poverty, Inequality and Development* (Cambridge University Press 1980) is a very important study of the development progress and growth strategies of a variety of Third World countries, suggesting that absolute poverty and relative inequality could be alleviated in both high and low growth economies and in both market-oriented and socialist countries.

6   See section 11 in chapter 14 for suggestions for further reading on the ethical objections to the market economy.

11

Marxism:
The Compulsion to Neighbourly Love

Maciej Pomian-Srzednicki and Alexander Tomský

Dialogue with Marx?

Alexander Solzhenitsyn, the winner of the 1983 Templeton Prize,[1] recently gave the following explanation for the great disasters which had befallen Russia: 'Men have forgotten God; that's why it all happened'.[2] The great disasters to which he was referring were, of course, the establishment of communist totalitarianism and its aftermath of repression and murder. Since atheism occupies a central and integrating part in the thought of both the communist, or Marxist, philosophers and the thought and practice of leaders in communist states[3] regardless of any differences between them, the logic of Solzhenitsyn's view may appear too obvious to merit any further consideration. Yet it is also true that large numbers of what appear to be genuine Christians today argue that a dialogue with Marxists can have the goal of 'enhancing human dignity, freedom, creativity, and wholeness'.[4] These progressive Christians base their argument on the idea that there is a Christian core behind the façade of atheism and simultaneously suggest that the political structures of communism are either rooted in the practices and traditions of Christianity or, more cautiously, are at least in some ways congruent with it.

If the progressive Christians were limited to the lunatic fringe of contemporary sectarianism their ideas would not merit discussion. However, it is precisely because these ideas have found their way into places far removed from the fringe that it is vital to examine them more closely. Especially important is the way in which the progressive Christian ideas can act as a key element in the mobilization of Christian support for a variety of left-wing and anti-democratic causes ranging from support for unilateral disarmament to the varying degrees of approval given to the Soviet Union's activities in the world. The most commonly used justification of the progressive position is that it is no more than the logical outcome of a totally consistent application of the Christian social teaching.

A lesson from history

For the moment let us digress by taking a brief look at some sixteenth-century progressives. We refer here to the Anabaptists, the sectarians who are known principally on account of their extraordinary violence. The millenial yearnings of the Anabaptists led them to abandon the fundamental teaching of Christ when he asserted, 'My kingdom is not of this world', and to establish their paradise in Münster. This paradise was one where each was expected to be righteous and love his neighbour under pain of death or exile. The community became reduced to a state where corruption and bestiality reigned supreme and very soon nothing was left except bones and ruins. The point of this example is to illustrate that attempts to *impose* Christian principles on a community or society can neither be called Christian nor be expected to have socially desirable effects. Leszek Kolakowski, the Polish philosopher, might have been thinking of the Anabaptists when he observed that:

> Communism believed that you can compel people to love one another — and that is a prescription for GULAG. We might find it appalling that free societies of the Western type are based on greed as the main human motivation, but this is still better than compulsory love, for that can only end in a society of prisoners and prison warders.[5]

We have illustrations here of how the freedom to be Christian depends on freedom to sin.

The acceptance of the imperfect world where the individual seeks to better himself through the love of God and of his neighbour is a fundamental principle implicit in all Christian tradition. It is by departing from this principle to a vision of a perfect social system in which any sort of personal betterment is irrelevant that the progressive Christian begins to secularize himself by undermining the very fundamentals of his own beliefs. Furthermore, the departure from this principle is in fact a loss of Christianity itself, for without the centrality of metaphysics Christianity is reduced to a mere set of social doctrines and becomes like a tree without roots. Once this principle is abandoned, these social doctrines of the progressives become fully congruent with Marxist doctrines; both seek to alter structures with varying degrees of violence and both seek to establish the temporal paradise. The teachings of Christ, however, point not in the direction of changing society but in the direction of changing the persons through a spiritual conversion; any lasting changes in society will ultimately depend on inner changes within individuals themselves. It would be wrong to conclude at this point, however, that human institutions cannot be improved or that their improvement is totally dependent on the goodness of the men running them. The central point is that no social improvement can be achieved through a master plan, simply because society consists of a multitude of individuals with a multitude of conflicting interests; the principle of the perfectibility of the person cannot be transferred onto society. Societies need compromise and can achieve only harmony.

The total loss of the metaphysical dimension in Christian ethics has been quite dramatically exemplified by the Catholic General Secretary of CND, Mgr Bruce Kent, who stated on Independent Radio News:

> If the Church is busy sitting in its sacristies counting its rosary beads and ignoring the great problems of the world then I don't think it's the right Church for me.[6]

It is clear that Mgr Kent, in total contrast with the Christian tradition, does not see any relationship between personal perfectibility through contemplative prayer and social problems.

Support for Communism

This sort of muddled thinking on the part of such Christians has some quite unfortunate practical consequences which we can clearly observe. Two examples are the support given to communist regimes and to communist-inspired liberation movements in Latin America. While it is possible to stress the differences between Eastern Europe and Latin America, the only difference between the two versions of support is a practical one: the first suggests joining hands with those who are already in power whilst the second encourages unity with political movements which still aspire to power.

What are the underpinnings of this quest for unification with Marxists? We might find one answer in the disaffected Christian who finds the application of Christian principles to himself in the imperfect world too difficult, and who consequently discovers that the Marxist utopia can deliver him from his predicament. He soon begins to identify Marxism with 'real Christianity'. The application of a concept of 'real Christianity' to the problems of society was already typical of the sectarian movements of the Middle Ages. Like the contemporary Marxist utopians, many of the sectarians had already been preoccupied with the idea of revolutionary change according to which the world is so evil that reform is mere tinkering and a total destruction and rebuilding of social relations offer the only hope. The real world thus becomes an object of hate as do those who offer any protest. This revolutionary element is neatly expressed in the tradition of the Anabaptists mentioned earlier, whose leader, Thomas Müntzer, outlined how priests and monks who objected to his version of Christianity should be treated: 'The sword is necessary to exterminate them'.[7] Generations later Lenin was to echo similar feelings by saying:

> The more representatives of the reactionary bourgeoisie and the reactionary clergy we manage to shoot the better.[8]

Because of Marxism's roots in the millennial sectarian tradition the sociology which is derived from it appears to slot neatly into Christian doctrine. The discovery that 'God is on the side of the poor'[9] is simply the progressives' appropriation of the Marxist concept of the historic role of the proletariat. The hypocrisy of the Latin American millionaire praying in church every Sunday is pointed to and it is repeated that he is beyond redemption. He is seen as the living example of the failure of traditional Christianity to solve the problem of poverty: the only way out is to put him out of his misery. The scene is thus set for a change in the social structures so that it can be demanded that neighbours be loved or else . . .

It follows, therefore, that to be on the side of the poor is to be on the side of God, in the same way as being on the side of the proletariat is accepting the inevitability of their historic role. The 'Liberation Theologians' are quite clear when they argue that to reject the demands of the poor is to reject God: 'Those who deny this deny the cause of Christ'.[10] This, of course, is not their plea for charity in the theological sense, but the application of a Marxist class analysis where God becomes embodied in the proletariat: hence its redeeming mission to liberate the whole of mankind. The plea is for a direct restructuring of society, even through violence, until there remains no differences between rich and poor. This is quite the opposite of charity. Christ himself referred to the problem of poverty when, on being questioned whether the expensive oil used to anoint him would not be better sold and the proceeds donated to the poor, he said, 'The poor you have always with you'.[11] Perhaps Christ himself might at some stage be seen to have failed.

Atheistic Marxism

The strong identification of God with history can also be found reduced to absurdity when even *atheism* is seen to be in some sense 'godly'. The argument here is, not that God is present *despite* atheism, but that he can actually manifest himself *in* atheism.[12] Once this is accepted the further acceptance of dialogue and co-operation with communist thinkers and communist leaders does not present any particular doctrinal problem.

The central issue connected with the anti-religious elements of theoretical Marxism and the similarly strong anti-religious policies of communist states can be conveniently avoided by seeing in them the hand of God. There are even suggestions that Christians in communist states should refrain from declaring their beliefs on the grounds that such declarations may 'provide material for further attacks on religion'.[13] Is this, Christians must ask, what Christ taught and is it this for which countless martyrs have died?

When Fidel Castro declared that 'Christ was a great revolutionary',[14] he was seeking the support of Christians although it is most unlikely that he would have placed Christ above himself in a league table of revolutionaries. Indeed, his statement makes no more sense than the suggestion that Che Guevara may be a great Christian.[15] Castro was expressing the same intentions as Stalin who, during the Second World War, called upon the Orthodox Church to mobilize the support of the Russian population against Hitler's armies. Those Christians who are unable to see beyond the rhetoric will never be able to understand the plight of

Christians in communist states (although this is well-documented) or even appreciate the coercive pressures which are brought to bear on beliefs in general. Under circumstances where Christian support is not required communist leaders are the first to assert their total commitment to an atheist society.

The ultimate absurdity of a Christian alliance with Marxists, however, lies in a total inability to understand the nature of militant atheism and its centrality within Marxism. This atheism is often mistaken for mere agnosticism or atheism by default. However, it goes much deeper than that. It rests on a conscious decision to 'liberate' people from the constraints of conscience, to make relative the timeless demands of truth, justice or even the customs and traditions of history, in order to become absolute masters of history. For a Christian, conscience is not a constraint but is moral instinct itself. In giving their support to Marxists, Christians are therefore committing not only a theological mistake but are also actively contributing to the destruction of their own beliefs. To claim at this stage that there is no need to worry because God is present even in militant atheism is to embrace the tradition that black is white and white is black. We must recognize this argument and treat it accordingly.

NOTES

1 The Templeton Prize was awarded tc Solzhenitsyn for his contributions to the 'renaissance of religion in atheistic nations'.

2 Alexander Solzhenitsyn, 'Godlessness, the First Step to Gulag' (The Templeton Address, Guildhall, London, 11 May 1983) p. 1.

3 cf. Maciej Pomian-Srzednicki, *Religious Change in Contemporary Poland* (Routledge & Kegan Paul 1982) esp. pp. 46-66.

4 Ans J. van der Bent, *Christians and Communists* (Geneva, World Council of Churches, 1980) p. 33. This view is typical of those held by members of the World Council of Churches and is also the sort of view to which Solzhenitsyn's strongly critical remarks were addressed when he said that the WCC remained 'blind and deaf to the persecution of religion in the USSR' (op. cit., p. 6).

5 George Urban, 'The Devil in History — A conversation with Leszek Kolakowski', *Encounter* (January 1981) no. 1, vol. LVI.

6 May 1 1983.

7 Norman Cohn, *The Pursuit of the Millennium* (Paladin 1970) p. 239.

8 *Spotkania* (London edition) 1977, no. 1, p. 82. *Spotkania* is a Polish periodical and is available at Keston College.

9   Fr Jean-Marie Tillard to an inter-American meeting of religious, November 1977. Quoted in *Religion and Freedom* (July 1978) p. 10.

10 Leonardo Boff, *Jesus Christ Liberator* (New York, Orbis Books, 1972) p. 95.

11 Mark 14.7.

12 For example Bruce Kenrick, *A Man from the Interior* (Epworth Press 1980) esp. pp. 52-6 and 114. Pastor Kenrick's book is about his visit to Castro's Cuba. It is perfectly clear that he sees the hand of God working through the Marxist regime.

13 Van der Bent, op. cit., p. 27.

14 During a visit to Jamaica, November 1977. Quoted in Edward Norman, *Christianity and the World Order* (OUP 1979) p. 43.

15 This is the message that Bruce Kenrick (op. cit., pp. 53-4) is intent on getting across. He begins by quoting his Cuban acquaintance and then adds his own comments: 'Many Christians here feel that Che is perhaps what Christ would have been in our time. He could be the twentieth-century image of God. Certainly, I reflected, Che showed many of the marks of Christ: poverty, suffering, being persecuted for the sake of justice, dying for others.'

12

Christian Socialism: An Old Heresy?

William Oddie

The divine bias

Is there a 'divine bias to the poor'? Does God's special blessing rest on a particular socio-economic class whose merit is that its members are materially 'deprived'; and is there a corresponding divine disfavour against the wealthy? Or are we to understand the expression 'the poor' in Jesus' teaching to imply some other teaching? For left-wing theologians the answer is clear: Jesus proclaims that the materially poor are especially favoured by God and that the wealthy are the enemies of his Kingdom. To look for some other meaning in his message is to 'spiritualize' the gospel.[1]

On what is this understanding based? In his book, *Bias to the Poor*, Bishop David Sheppard helpfully offers five proof texts[2] which, he believes, establish clearly that in Jesus' teaching, the expression 'the poor' carries clearly and unambiguously an economic meaning: 'the poor' are the *materially* poor. These texts (RSV) are as follows:

1   *Matthew 11.5* The blind receive their sight and the lame walk, lepers are cleansed and the deaf hear, and the dead are raised up, and the poor have good news preached to them.

2   *Mark 10.25* It is easier for a camel to go through the eye of a needle than for a rich man to enter the kingdom of God.

3   *Luke 4.18* The Spirit of the Lord is upon me, because he has anointed me to preach good news to the poor. He has sent me to proclaim release to the captives and recovering of sight to the blind, to set at liberty those who are oppressed . . .

4   *Luke 6.20* Blessed are you poor, for yours is the kingdom of God.

5   *Luke 6.24* But woe to you that are rich, for you have received your consolation.

Removed from their biblical context and projected through the lens of a modern socialist political consciousness, these passages, assembled in this way, certainly appear to provide an impressive body of supporting evidence for Bishop Sheppard's contention. How does his use of this particular collection of texts withstand closer examination?

Biblical basis for favouring the 'poor'?

Four of the five texts, all except 2, quote from or refer to a single Old Testament text,[3] and Luke 4.18, of course, shows Jesus reading it aloud in the synagogue: afterwards he proclaims 'today this scripture has been fulfilled in your hearing' (4.21). The text is from Isaiah 61.1-2:

> The spirit of the Lord God is upon me,
> because the Lord has anointed me
> to bring good tidings to the afflicted;
> he has sent me to bind up the broken-hearted,
> to proclaim liberty to the captives,
> and the opening of the prison to those who are bound;
> to proclaim the year of the Lord's favour,
> and the day of vengeance of our God;
> to comfort all who mourn . . .

Luke's text is in fact a conflation of this passage with another (Isaiah 58.6); this enables him to emphasize the theme of *release*, a word to be understood in the sense of forgiveness from sin (an essential Lucan theme).[4] The basic text, from Isaiah 61.1ff, clearly identifies the poor in this context as the 'afflicted', or 'poor' in the sense of 'pious', as those described by Professor Geoffrey Lampe, writing on Luke 6.20, as 'the typical saints of Judaism, the poor, humble and pious'.[5] In Matthew's version of this beatitude they are described as 'the poor in spirit'; the New English Bible (2nd edn) helpfully translates this as 'those who know their need of God. (Matt. 5.3). Very strangely, Bishop Sheppard accepts this interpretation for Matthew's version, but claims Luke's as one of the texts where 'the plain meaning is that Jesus is talking about the materially poor'.[6] What he does *not* mention is that they are in fact simply different versions of the *same saying*.[7] Luke 6.20 is in fact one of those texts of which it is important clearly to understand, as the New Testament scholar Alan Richardson put it, 'that the words "poor" and "rich" have in many contexts a religious and ethical content rather than an economic one'. Richardson identifies Luke's 'blessed are you poor' as having such a content, and continues:

> Jesus means 'the poor' in the sense in which the term is used as a technical expression in later Jewish literature, as denoting the class of pious, hard-working, humble folk who look to God for redemption and who do not put their trust in political schemes or material prosperity: theirs, says Jesus, is the kingdom of God.[8]

The 'rich' by antithesis (as in Luke 6.24) are the arrogant, those confident in their own strength, who insist on knowing God, if at all, on *their* terms rather than on his.[9]

Textual Exegesis in the service of political radicalism

The misuse of such texts for the purposes of a merely political radicalism is most notable, perhaps, among socialists, but is by no means confined to them. David Steel, the leader of the British Liberal party, for instance, invited by the *Church Times* to identify the specifically Christian aspects of his party's philosophy, asserted that:

> The gospel is radical and disturbing in its implications — there can be no possible doubt about that; and it is a denial of its truth to try to 'spiritualize'. The parable of Dives and Lazarus, the sermon on the Mount, Our Lady's words in the *Magnificat* about God putting down the mighty from their seat and exalting the humble and meek offer very little comfort to the members of the Conservative Party . . . Not for nothing did Bernard Shaw say that the *Magnificat* was more revolutionary than the *Internationale*.[10]

The *Magnificat* is, perhaps, the most frequently misused text of all. Shaw here (followed by Steel, Bishop Sheppard and a wearisome list of others) imputes to the Mother of Christ revolutionary political beliefs on the strength of three verses (Luke 1.51-3):

> He has scattered the proud in the imagination of their hearts,
> he has put down the mighty from their thrones,
> and exalted those of low degree;
> he has filled the hungry with good things,
> and the rich he has sent empty away.

Like the *Benedictus* (Luke 1.68-79), which it parallels, the
Magnificat is made up of Old Testament quotations; it recalls
particularly the Song of Hannah (1 Sam. 2.1-10),[11] and the verses
just quoted derive from the following (vv. 6-8a):

> The Lord kills and brings to life;
> he brings down to Sheol and raises up.
> The Lord makes poor and makes rich;
> he brings low, he also exalts.
> He raises up the poor from the dust;
> he lifts the needy from the ash heap,
> to make them sit with princes
> and inherit a seat of honour . . .

The passage as a whole is a hymn of praise to God, who controls
life and death and the vagaries of human fortune; it ends with the
assertion that he 'will give strength to his king, and raise high the
head of his anointed prince'. The reference here is to the monarchy
of Saul and David: the song, thus, is very far from preaching
equality; it asserts that it is God only who in the end confers rank
and wealth, the possession of which with his favour is both
desirable and legitimate. Mary's own song may clearly not be
legitimately interpreted in any radically different way. Her own
Son, though born in great humility, will be raised high by him
alone who gives greatness and power. It is manifestly not the
purpose of Mary's song to modify the Old Testament teaching
(implicit in 1 Samuel 2) that wealth, though evil if gained by
injustice (Isaiah 5.8) and spiritually dangerous if it leads to pride
and rebellion against God, may nevertheless also be a sign of
God's favour: Abraham, we are told, was 'very rich in cattle and
in silver and gold' (Genesis 13.2); Isaac (Genesis 26.12f) and
Jacob (Genesis 30.43) are similarly recipients of God's favour. In
the New Testament, we can see Joseph of Arimathaea as the type
of the wealthy though virtuous Jew. Despite his riches (Matthew
27.57) he was 'a good and righteous man' (Luke 23.50); and we
may see his gift of the tomb in which Our Lord's body lay for
three days as perhaps the most moving of all the many examples
recorded by history of the sanctification of personal wealth to the
purposes of God.

Mr Steel, St Augustine and the Sicilian Briton

The example of Abraham amusingly reminds us of Mr Steel's incautious interpretation of the parable of Dives and Lazarus as a story about the innate evil of riches. Assertions that the possession of wealth is contrary to the spirit of the gospel are, of course, by no means new; St Irenaeus,[12] St Clement of Alexandria[13] and other Fathers of the second century were in no doubt as to the danger of riches. But they have also emanated from less orthodox quarters, and in a very particular way which casts some light on our present inquiry. In the year 414, St Augustine found it necessary to refute a heretical writer known as the Sicilian Briton, who was teaching, according to Hilarius, a perplexed Sicilian Christian, that 'a rich man who continues to live rich cannot enter the kingdom of heaven unless he sells all that he has, and that it cannot do him any good to keep the commandments while keeping his riches'.[14]

St Augustine's counterblast was crisp and unhesitating: after reminding his correspondent of the riches of the Hebrew Patriarchs, he launches straight into a discussion of the parable of Dives and Lazarus. If Dives had shown mercy to the poor man, he would himself have deserved mercy:

> And if the poor man's merit had been his poverty, not his goodness, he surely would not have been carried by angels into the bosom of Abraham who had been rich in this life. This is intended to show us that on the one hand it was not poverty itself that was divinely honoured, nor, on the other, riches that were condemned, but that the godliness of the one and the ungodliness of the other had their own consequences, and, as the torment of fire was the lot of the ungodly rich man, so the bosom of the rich Abraham received the godly poor man. Although Abraham lived as a rich man, he held his riches . . . lightly . . .[15]

He held his riches lightly: here is the key to the meaning of Bishop Sheppard's remaining 'proof' text (no. 2) from Mark 10.25. This saying refers, of course, to the story of the rich young ruler which immediately precedes it. Perceiving that for him too close an attachment to his possessions has become spiritually dangerous, Jesus calls the young man not simply to obedience to the law but to perfection; For him, this will mean the renunciation of his wealth. But as Dr Robert Wilson points out:

> the 'counsel of perfection' should not be generalised: this was the crucial test in this particular case, but the barrier in other cases may be different.[16]

The saying about the camel and the needle's eye which follows this has attracted a number of interpretations; according to one, for instance, the needle's eye is the pedestrian gate of a Palestinian walled town where after nightfall when the main gate was shut, the camels would have to be unloaded and enter kneeling: a vivid image for humility and spiritual detachment from possessions. This interpretation finds little support from modern commentators, but it remains at the very least not incongruous with the saying's context and meaning. Wilson, however, rightly says that any such possibility should not be used to weaken the saying which is 'a vivid hyperbole to express what is *humanly* impossible'.[17]

And here, we approach the crux of the matter. It is the question of what is humanly possible and what humanly impossible which is at the heart of the controversy between Augustine and the Sicilian Briton. It is this which gives this dispute its striking relevance to the debate in which the authors of this book are engaged. The Sicilian Briton was a militant protagonist of a heretical tendency known today as Pelagianism, named after a British monk, Pelagius. The Pelagians believed, briefly, that our own sinfulness is ultimately under our own control. We can *decide* to be sinless; and by our own effort we can achieve salvation. The chief obstacles to this are our own habits and settled dispositions which may be changed by an effort of will, and our surrounding environment, which can be changed by social reform. Our sinfulness is not inherent in the nature with which we are born into the world. On the contrary, the inherent goodness of human nature is the fundamental teaching of Pelagian philosophy.

Christian socialism as extreme Pelagianism

The beliefs of Pelagius were quickly taken up by others more extreme, notably the Sicilian Briton. For him, social reform had a quite clear meaning: 'abolish the rich'. To those who argued that it was impossible to give to the poor if no one possessed the necessary superfluity of worldly goods from which to give (an argument not wholly unlike the more developed modern Tory belief that only by removing obstacles to the creation of wealth can the economy fund necessary welfare spending), he replies, strikingly, by asserting a necessary structural connection between poverty and the existence of the wealthy:

> They do not understand that the reason why the poor exist is that the rich own too much. Abolish the rich and you will have no more poor. If no one has more than he needs, then everyone will have as much as he needs. For it is the few rich who are the cause of the many poor.[18]

This is, for its times, a startling analysis; it does not simply *remind* us of modern socialism: as John Morris comments of the Sicilian Briton's teachings as a whole,

> The crisp argumentation that wealth and property had arisen in the past through 'oppression'; that the existence of the rich, the fact that society is divided into such 'genera', is the cause of poverty, cruelty and violence; and that society should be wholly reshaped, now and in this present substance, by abolishing the rich and redistributing their property to the poor — is by any textbook definition socialism. Further it is socialism of a coherence and urgency that was hardly to be met again before the nineteenth century . . .[19]

It is when we understand the rootedness of these writings in their author's general theological presuppositions about the nature of man and the means of salvation that the parallels with much modern Christian socialism become most striking and most illuminating. There are differences, notably perhaps in the strong Pelagian emphasis on personal discipline. Nevertheless, the parallels remain sufficiently arresting. The tendency of Christian socialism to locate sin within the external 'structures of oppression' rather than in the relationship of fallen individuals (social beings, undoubtedly, but still individuals) with God; a strong instinct towards belief in the innate goodness of the human race, a goodness distorted only by the weight of the past and the pressures of external environment; the idea that the Kingdom of God is attainable by the assertion of the human will: all these ideas and tendencies are strongly reminiscent of that heresy whose spiritual dangers Augustine rightly perceived and vigorously fought.

Christianity and Marxism

It needs to be said, of course, that some Christian socialists would not accept this description of their beliefs; and Bishop Sheppard, for instance, has even criticized Marxist Christianity, asserting that 'when political liberation has come, there will still be inside people's hearts and minds greed, the will to dominate, irresponsibility'.[20] It remains uncertain whether such respectable Christian fellow-travellers have really grasped the transformation of their theological understanding that has actually taken place, whether or not they are still able to accept the traditional formulae which still give so much Christian socialism the appearance of doctrinal orthodoxy. For all his differences of emphasis with 'liberation' theologians, Bishop Sheppard is still prepared to propose the following beliefs as 'common ground' between Christianity and Marxism:

> The realisation that the economic and social structures of society can form the minds and shape the destinies of those who are subject to them.
>
> The questioning of who controls the means of production, and to whom they are accountable.
>
> An indignation at unequal distribution of wealth and opportunity.
>
> A belief in a better future order.
>
> A longing for a realistic programme, which the poor especially can strive after.[21]

The real problem is not whether these propositions are Christian in the sense that it is acceptable, even normal, for a Christian to hold them, in the sense that we may properly say that Nazism is *not* Christian. Certainly, the first article of belief here needs some qualification to allow for the grace of God acting in individual human lives — a significant (and characteristically Pelagian) omission. This proviso aside, it seems clear enough that there is no intrinsic incompatibility between these beliefs and the teachings of Jesus; but what is equally clear is that there is no pressing obligation on a Christian to profess them, either. The simple fact is that there is no *necessary* point of contact whatever between Bishop Sheppard's list of social and economic beliefs and the teachings of Christ, just as there is nothing in common, say, between the drama of William Shakespeare and the economics of John Maynard Keynes, though there is nothing abnormal or intolerably irrational in approving of both. Quite simply, there is a radical discontinuity between their nature, content, and purpose. The Bishop has simply made a list of Marxist beliefs and declared them Christian. It is a classic example of a now depressingly familiar characteristic of much Christian thought in the twentieth century, the absorption of theology by politics and economics and the location of Christian hope entirely within the possibilities (real or imagined) for human society. Entirely absent is the Christian longing for what lies beyond the world of sense, the knowledge of exile from the presence of God, which has been one mark of Christian spirituality through the ages. 'Here we have no abiding city', writes the author of Hebrews; 'but we seek one that is to come'. For Bishop Sheppard this is, doubtless, a text about urban reclamation; for him the 'belief in a better future order' has been focused clearly on political 'liberation', though, to be sure, he leaves room for a kind of spiritual mopping-up operation to take place afterwards.

Committed Christian but an unpoliticized Church

In 1928, Bishop Charles Gore looked back with some dissatisfaction, on the progress of the Christian Socialist movement in which he had for so many years been involved. There had, he thought, been a lack of certainty about methods and objectives.

> Thus — to name only one point, though a most important one — we are embarrassed by an uncertainty as to what the principles of Christ, such as admit of being applied to society, really were and are.

For the Christian Socialists of our own day, such uncertainties have melted away; though not, one may be very sure, in a way calculated to lessen Bishop Gore's embarrassment: already he was adding 'militant socialists' to those he believed 'grossly misrepresented' Our Lord.[22]

To assert that there is no way in which we can deduce an ideal political system or economic doctrine from the teachings of Christ is *not*, it cannot be emphasized too strongly, to say that Christian people should withdraw into an unhealthy pietism, which is the standard counter-accusation. It is simply to assert the profound dangers for the Church, speaking as the Church, to identify herself and her teachings with any particular political analysis. Most obviously, as William Temple pointed out, because any such identification might well be falsified by History.[23] Even more, as he went on to assert,

> is it a matter of justice, for even though a large majority of Christians hold a particular view, the dissentient minority may be equally loyal to Christ and equally entitled to be recognised as loyal members of his Church.

And so it is, when he offers his own detailed proposals for a welfare state, that Temple makes it very clear that he is doing so 'in [his] capacity as a Christian citizen'. And he goes on to say, in words which should be carved in stone above the entrance to every episcopal residence:

> If any member of the convocation of York should be so ill-advised as to table a resolution that these proposals be adopted as a political programme for the Church, I should as Archbishop resist that proposal with all my force, and should probably as President of the Convocation, rule it out of order. The Church is committed to the everlasting gospel and to the Creeds which formulate it; it must never commit itself to an ephemeral programme of detailed action.[24]

Now, forty years later, the Church appears less and less committed to its historic faith, more and more dogmatically committed precisely to ephemeral programmes of detailed action. It may only be when history has begun to deliver its judgement on such programmes that the bland certitude of their ecclesiastical protagonists will begin to waver. By then, alas for many Christian souls, it may be too late.

NOTES

1 D. Sheppard, *Bias to the Poor* (1983) pp. 12-14.

2 ibid., p. 14 n6, listed on p. 227.

3 M. Black, ed., *Peake's Commentary on the Bible* (1962) 783, § 684a for Matt. 11.5 (K. Stendhal); p. 827, § 722d for Luke 4.18 and p. 830,

§ 724i for Luke 6.20 and 24 (G. W. H. Lampe). My biblical exegesis will generally conform with that of the authors of *Peake's Commentary*, both for the texts already mentioned and for others to which they are related. This will ensure an independently determined selection of supporting biblical authorities, and one thus immune from any suggestion of political bias.

4   ibid., p. 828, § 722g.

5   ibid., p. 830, § 724i.

6   Sheppard, op. cit., p. 14 n6.

7   Peake, p. 830, § 724i.

8   A. Richardson, ed., *Theological Word Book of the Bible* (1950) pp. 168-9.

9   ibid.

10 *Church Times* (June 3 1983) p. 11.

11 Peake, p. 825, § 710, h, i.

12 Irenaeus, *Adversus Haereses,* ed. Harvey, iv. 30.i,ii. 248.

13 See J. Morris, 'Pelagian Literature', *Journal of Theological Studies,* NS Vol. XVI, Pt 1 (April 1965) p. 44.

14 R. J. Deferrari, ed. (trans. W. Parsons), *Saint Augustine's Letters, III* (1953), *Ep.* 156, 318.

15 ibid., *Ep.* 157, 340-1.

16 Peake, p. 811, § 706c.

17 ibid.

18 Morris, op. cit., p. 50.

19 ibid., pp. 50-1.

20 Sheppard, op. cit., p. 154.

21 ibid., p. 151.

22 C. Gore, *Christ and Society* (1928) p. 19.

23 W. Temple, *Christianity and Social Order* (1976) pp. 40-41.

24 ibid., p. 41.

13

The Church of England:
From Established Church to Secular Lobby

David Martin

This chapter, like others, is concerned with the Church of England's disposition to a specific social issue — its relationship to public and national matters. But unlike them, this disposition is not to be found in succinct statements but in various attitudes and trends of the contemporary Church. The Church of England, or some of its members, is uneasy about some of the ways in which it has historically related to this country. In the first place, though disestablishment is only desired by a minority, the Church increasingly thinks of itself as a private association, run by a modern bureaucracy. In the second place, many churchmen dislike being part of a Ministry of Ceremonies, decorating the state. In the third place, there is a feeling which suspects the special link with *this* land, *this* place, *this* people. And in the fourth place, the Church of fact and history is partly dissolving into a Church of opinions, not so much nourishing personal and corporate devotion, as exerting pressure for changes in political and social structures. This pressure may or may not be justified, morally and as practical politics, but it is clear that ecclesiastical spokesmen often do not represent the viewpoint of the laity.

My interest centres on the way that this peculiar and special institution, the C. of E., understands and is related to the *res publica*. By *res publica* I mean the settled forms of the constitution, the modes of government, both ceremonial and practical, the sense of ethnic identity which achieves some defined presence in the public forum, and the issues therein debated. I have some very simple theses to advance with respect to changes now evident in the way the Church understands its relationship to the constitution, to government, to the English people and England, and to the issues of the day.

From establishment to private association

So far as the constitution is concerned, especially the 'established' position of the Church, there is no great disposition among the majority to change it, whether we speak of the clergy or the laity. There is, however, a minority, probably located for the most part among activist members of the Church, which at least contemplates disestablishment. It does so for two reasons, one being that the Church cannot properly develop its political views while retaining the established connection, and the other being that the Church must have complete authority to order its own affairs. Clearly, not all those minded to pursue disestablishment would give both reasons, and I suspect that those who want simply to be supreme in what they regard as their 'own' house outnumber those who think that the Church can gain some new freedom to adopt radical politics.

This is not the place to consider what is implied by such a notion as being supreme in one's 'own' house. I have put the word 'own' in inverted commas to indicate how peculiar it is historically for the Church to be regarded as a private association under the aegis of some specialized bureaucracy, which speaks 'for' it. I will, however, note one oddity, before passing on. The term 'the Church' as deployed by the bureaucracy, and also as appropriated by the General Synod, continues to carry a traditional meaning, as denoting the *corpus Christianorum* or 'the body of all faithful people'. But this traditional usage only conceals a non-traditional intention, which is to attach the label 'the Church' to the opinions of a bureaucratically organized pressure group, especially as embodied in its specialist agencies. To use the velvet glove of tradition to cover the hand of a pressure group is quite characteristic of the whole style of today's Church of England.

An end to the 'ministry of ceremonies'

So much for my first thesis. My second thesis concerns the modes of government, more especially the ceremonial aspect of power and national fraternity. At one level this has to do with expressions of the authority of Queen-in-Parliament. At another level, it has to do with expressions of locality, local government and local dignity. The constitutional theorist Walter Bagehot distinguished between the dignified and the efficient parts of the constitution, and the Church has offered a service (in both senses of the word 'service') more particularly to the dignified part. However, this distinction is misleading if we take it to mean that the Queen and the Church are so much stucco providing external ornament to the edifice of 'real' government. True, the Queen *reigns* but does not *rule*, but the enactments and rituals of Queen and Church, and Queen-in-Parliament have their own 'efficiency' as much as the day-to-day enactments of the legislature. Indeed, great affection and loyalty are accorded to this 'dignity', and to the formulae of the state. Seals, stamps, insignia, colours, honours, and memorials of war, are nearly all cast in this frame. 'Dignity' after all derives from *'dignus'* and means worth, or worthiness. In an intangible way this 'worth' is attached to two *personal* institutions, a royal family, and a body, the Church which uses the personal images of Father, Son and Mother in the language of devotion. Of course, such loyalties are hedged around with *scepticisms*, vague *suspicions* of pomp and show, utilitarian *dislike* of ritual or radical contempt (and *envy*) of wealth, and these doubts may well be more vigorous with regard to Church than to Monarchy. All the same, the ambivalence towards the idea of worth or 'dignity' associated with Monarch and Church has to be set against the background of a much greater scepticism about politicians and the political apparatus. On the one hand, the clergyman is often a figure of fun on the media, portrayed as a 'goonish' idiot with a funny voice; on the other hand, polls also show him as somebody, like the Queen, usually thought to be 'doing a good job'.

This, as I have said, has everything to do with *res publica*, which may include royal marriages, state funerals, monuments in Westminster Abbey to Darwin, the Wesleys, or Handel, the annual services which take place at the Cenotaph in Whitehall and in every town and village in November. The link of the Church with the public forum surfaces in the prayers said every day before Parliament begins, and the 'state prayers' in the Book of Common Prayer.

How, then, does the contemporary C. of E. regard this 'service' to the *res publica*? Well, to adapt a phrase from Karl Marx, there are many churchmen who regard the service of the Church to the whole public domain as washing dirty political linen in holy water, a sort of distracting and deluding asperges to what *really* goes on. There are a lot of reasons for this, and there is no way in which we can quantify precisely how many churchmen entertain how many, and with what degree of intensity.

One reason lies in the difference between the declining position of the clergy, socially and educationally, and their honorific role. Many in the Church feel that to play a part in certain carefully arranged but limited state performances is to act as the derisory lackeys of power. They feel out of place, almost manipulated for public purposes, and otherwise treated as of no account or, even worse, as members of a biddable department of state. There are clergy who deeply resent being officials in what they regard as a 'Ministry of Ceremonies'. Beyond that, they suspect ritual and ceremony as such, whether in state or in Church. They contrast the inwardness of the Christian religion with the externals and rigidities of public roles. This inwardness is linked to modern cults of the informal, in manners, dress and deportment. Public matters are defined and suspected as 'matters of form'.

It is believed, rightly or wrongly, that the benefits of association with power are outweighed by the costs of the Church being identified with a 'Them' against a popular 'Us'. This belief not only generates gestures of dis-association but probably provides a special frisson for some of those who step 'out of line' to challenge some aspect of public policy or what are thought to be established, accepted mores. Indeed, this stepping 'out of line' has now become so fashionable and frequent, that today's 'nonconformists' are those who maintain the old position. It is impossible to determine the complicated motivations of those representing the new consensus. No doubt there is genuine sympathy for the disadvantaged (or 'bias towards the poor' in the phrase of the Bishop of Liverpool) intermingled with the resentments of a *declassé* clerical class, and the tendency of some clergy to repeat the shibboleths of yesterday's intelligentsia.

Of course, there are certain ancient tensions given new life by current conditions. One is the remnant of lay patronage. Another is the way the aristocracy has sometimes seen the clergy as existing to provide a purely 'spiritual' support for social caste, and moreover, as composed of those whose talents are too exiguous for them to survive elsewhere. Whatever the precise mix of idealism, of resentment, and of deference to yesterday's secular humanist fashion, there is little doubt that the Church is now deeply ambivalent about its ceremonial role in the public domain.

There are various indicators of this ambivalence. One is a form of neo-clericalism which would like to dramatize the problem in terms of Caesar and God, as if Caesar straightforwardly represented the profane political powers of this world and the Church were straightforwardly God's champion. The Reverend Colin Buchanan has expressed himself precisely in these terms. Neo-clericalist sentiment lies behind the promotion of the clergy over against the monarchy in the new liturgy, and in a studied omission in many services of the state prayers. It is, perhaps, useful to remember that not all assertions of clerical independence are idealistically motivated, though some undoubtedly are. The Oxford Movement, for example, in part focused the desire for clerical autonomy around the way a lay government insisted on reforming the corrupt Church of Ireland. Equivalent resentments were recently expressed at the very idea that Parliament might through a Prayer Book (Protection) Bill shore up the exiguous rights of traditionally minded laity against impositions by clerical modernizers.

Why England and the English people in particular?

Many of the elements just referred to play into my third thesis, which concerns Church and people. The geographical roots of the Church of England, staked out in locality and nation, symbolized in a vast architectural deposit, including 11,000 medieval churches, is widely held to be an embarrassment. Indeed, the Church is ambivalent towards culture in both senses of the word: the way of life of a distinctive, historic entity — England — and the qualitative achievements of Englishmen. The very idea of a national church is regarded as inextricably connected with ethnocentric attitudes and chauvinistic ambitions. Modern man is held to be on the move, dis-located, and the Church should mirror his rejection of specific attachments and of long-term roots. This theology of displacement is extended further to include a negative attitude towards buildings and their capacity to act as markers. The parish church ministry is for unexciting generalists, tending a dying folk religiosity. By contrast the specialist ministries are for those who want to be on the move.

The consequences which this Christian version of the displaced, or rather 'unplaced', person has for any concern about *res publica* are clear. The very notion of a specific mission to *this* island and *this* people can be regarded as a contravention of the universality of the gospel. The 'scandal of particularity' which used to be proudly affirmed with regard to a theology of the incarnation in time and place, is shamefacedly avoided with regard to the particularity of the mission of the Church of England. At the same time, such a mission is seen as ecumenically offensive, in spite of the fact that the Roman Church in Poland and in Southern Ireland acts as *the* national Church. Indeed, even in England Roman Catholicism has acted as a guardian of the ethnic identity of eight million people of Irish descent, not to mention migrant Poles, Hungarians, Italians, and so on who are now permanent citizens.

Ecumenism is held to supersede all special missions, and the way in which particular traditions have acquired roots in specific soils over millennia. The politics of ecumenism are here supported by sociological analyses of the dissolution of the ancient tie of faith and peoplehood. I would not deny the solvents which attack this tie, and I have myself analysed them in *Daedalus*.[1] My emphasis at this point is on the dislike of the very idea of 'emplacement' most obvious amongst those whose historic task has been to extend and cherish roots.

There is a very awkward area here which the Church of England explores with some uneasiness and that is the relationship between the unique particularity of the Monarchy, and the Church, of which the Monarch is Supreme Governor. The Queen is not *summus episcopus*, but her person is integrally bound up with the special role of *the* national Church and with the part it plays in the *res publica*. There have been critical murmurings about the law guaranteeing the Protestant succession, but nobody has yet tried to work out the constitutional upheaval which would follow were the Church of England in any way to accept the jurisdiction of Rome. (I may add that I believe this very unlikely, short of an equivalent upheaval in Rome. I say this in no party spirit or out of disrespect for other traditions, but merely as a judgement of social fact.)

Of course, the tendencies of the last two centuries, at least up to the events in Teheran, suggest that the state will increasingly

139

be non-confessional. Mr Benn, on the Labour left, may be merely anticipating the next instalment of that trend in demanding the denationalization of the Church. But if this is so, it does not follow that the connection between a Church and a people, a tradition and a people, is therefore severed. Witness Poland.

From individual devotion to criticism of social structures

My fourth thesis concerns a trend which I have elsewhere described as a shift from an emphasis on the individual in his particular situation to an analysis in terms of social structural defects. As a sociologist I am not disposed to underplay the sedimentation of action in structures of roles and of institutions. Charles Sisson writing in *Anglican Essays*[2] has expressed the matter in a different, but parallel way. In his view the emphasis on individual conscience, which was uniquely achieved in Anglo-Saxon cultures, has been subtly revamped as the collection and advancement of *opinions* about what *somebody else* ought to be doing or have done. Guilt no longer inheres in the responsible person, but in blameworthy collectivities. Christian examination of the self is thus transformed into a giving forth of opinions, vaguely certified as of Christian provenance.

These opinions emanate in particular from precisely those bureaucracies and their specialist agencies which nowadays (in defiance of the new theology of the *laos*) refer to themselves as 'the Church' and their opinions as 'the mind of the Church'. This is not to say that such agencies must be mistaken, or inevitably ill-informed, though their views may not always take fully into account the normal and very real constraints of political action. It is to reiterate, however, that they do not necessarily carry their constituencies with them. All the same, they do influence a particular group of those who form opinion, and in a vague way this influence is then disseminated further under the aegis of the presumed moral authority of the appointed guardians of the faith. Certainly the present government has taken certain of the opinions advanced, particularly on matters of defence, with sufficient seriousness to argue against them, and (perhaps) even to bethink how best to ensure more amenable church appointments in the future.

From one point of view, this constant busyness in the forming and issuing of opinions really further emphasizes how the Church acts now as a pressure group presenting 'Christian' approaches to *res publica* and the issues of the public forum. Certainly the General Synod, sensitive to its autonomy, sees itself in the model of a mini-Parliament, issuing statements, even though it is not democratically elected and is only incidentally 'representative'. This is all of a piece with the view which regards the raw material of liturgy as found in today's (and therefore yesterday's) newspaper. Opinion is understood as 'prophecy'. Political action is seen as providing instalments of the Kingdom of God, and 'progress' is assimilated to the advent of the Kingdom of God.

Charles Sisson, in the essays referred to above, puts the traditional alternative to this quite succinctly.

> The slightly flabby tentacles of the church stretched out into the ordinary population, and it was by no means clear where they stopped ... With the sharp decline in the intellectual calibre of the clergy ... the strong intellectual case for the soggy middle — the historical case — fell by the wayside ... What we have now, instead of a *via media*, is a sort of canting conspiracy of the more superficial elements in both ecclesiastical wings, a church of *opinion* rather than of fact and history ... The whole tone of the Church of England is now that of a sect ... The proper Anglican view of these matters ... is that the church instructs its man, makes what it can of him in the circle of its devotions, and then leaves him to go out and play his part in the commonwealth as best he can and as his own peculiar knowledge and experience, whatever they may be, suggest.[3]

Now, this analysis, though evaluative in its judgements, can be recast as a straightforward statement of what is socially the case as regards the sectarian drift of the national Church.

All I have said up to this point could be rephrased in sociological terminology; the plurality of options in modern society, the left-liberal tendencies in the expressive professions, the marginalization of ecclesiastical bodies, the bureaucratic oligarchies which emerge even in Christian 'pressure groups', the secularization of the state, in its efficient and dignified parts, the separation of *regio* and *religio*, peoplehood and the faith. But whether one employs technical terminology or ordinary discourse, the same trends emerge.

How the demotion of the Prayer Book focuses these trends

I have indicated several tendencies: away from historic and local roots, and away from the *res publica*, towards the politics of a private association pursued at the widest level in international groupings like the W.C.C. I will conclude by noting one issue which has brought several of these tendencies into play. I do not intend to analyze it now.

The issue has to do with the alterations made to the historic liturgy. The demotion of the liturgy was, in my view, precisely an attempt to avoid or repudiate 'culture' in both senses of the word, to escape the toils of a national mission, to upgrade the clergy vis-à-vis the regal emphasis of the older formularies. Perhaps above all it was an attempt to assert the autonomous powers of those running a private religious association over against those in Parliament who were elected by the whole Commonwealth, using the word 'Commonwealth' in the ancient sense intended by Richard Hooker in 'Of the Laws of Ecclesiastical Polity'. This clericalization of a once comprehensive body, and this self-willed as well as socially-propelled adoption of the style of a 'gathered' church, involves a clash both with the older landed and political élites, and with a significant segment of the academic and intellectual presence in England, Christian and secular. There remains in the universities what has partly disappeared from the Church: a sense of guardianship embodied in Coleridge's notion of 'the clerisy'. 'The clerisy' was thought by Coleridge to concern itself with richness of historical accumulation, and especially with the *res publica*. The repudiation of the historic liturgy, coextensive in its creation with the highest energies of the English language, was in part a concentrated symbolic repudiation of the relation between Church and Christian Commonwealth, and a way of signalling a mood of withdrawal from the things which pertain to the public realm, the *res publica*.

NOTES

1   D. Martin, 'Revived Dogma and New Cult', *Daedalus* (Winter 1982) pp. 53-72.
2   C. Sisson, *Anglican Essays* (Carcanet New Press 1983).
3   Ibid., p. 106-7.

14

Sources for a More Balanced Discussion of Socio-Economic Issues

Rachel Steare

Introduction

Two entirely different moods periodically descend upon the researcher in economics and religion: one is despair at the vast expanse of ignorance that generally surrounds discussion of the relationship between culture and economic life in both religious and secular circles: the other is amazement at the wealth of material (much of it recently published) that exists to throw light on this subject but which is so frequently ignored in the writings and pronouncements of churchmen and others who concern themselves with such matters.

This brief bibliographical survey is intended to give some indication of the range of resources available to those who feel that the currently popular social and economic orthodoxies (whether those espoused by the Christian left or the Christian right) leave something to be desired. It is inevitably highly selective and does no more than reflect the extent and limitations of one person's interest and reading.

The material can be divided into two broad groupings: firstly, those writings that examine various aspects of the Christian critique of capitalism, whether from a positive or negative point of view; and secondly, those that explore the role of religion, and of cultural values more generally, in economic life.

Christian critiques of capitalism — sources

A useful introduction to some of the intellectual and psychological sources of contemporary opposition to capitalism, both within the Church and beyond, is provided by two anthologies of essays by leading economists, sociologists and theologians, published in 1979. In a volume entitled *Capitalism: Sources of Hostility,* Ernest van den Haag of the Heritage Foundation in New York has

143

drawn together seven essays that reach beyond the intellectual debate about the advantages and demerits of the market economy, to probe some of the emotional and non-rational sources of hostility towards capitalism — such as fear of the freedom and responsibility produced by the expansion of consumer choice within a free market system. Included in the collection is an essay by Peter Bauer on the origins of Third World antagonism towards the market and the phenomenon of Western guilt about Third World poverty. The debate aroused on both sides of the Atlantic by Edward Norman's 1977 lecture, 'The Denigration of Capitalism', has prompted the publication by the American Enterprise Institute of a collection of papers by four American theologians, commenting on Norman's argument that the anti-capitalist bias of British intellectual culture has been responsible for the 'moral subversion' of free society. Edited by Michael Novak, *The Denigration of Capitalism: Six Points of View*, includes a reprint of Edward Norman's original lecture.

Roots of anti-capitalism

Another exposé of the roots of anti-capitalist thinking is found in Paul Johnson's *Enemies of Society*, published in 1978 by Weidenfeld and Nicolson. An opening historical survey of Western economic development is followed by a characteristically vigorous assessment of the role played in the assault on freedom by what this former editor of the *New Statesman* terms the purveyors of 'ecological panic' and other unreal and unreasonable fears of economic growth.

Myths in Third World views

From the same publisher come three books by Peter Bauer of the London School of Economics, challenging from an economist's standpoint some widely held views about poverty and economic development. Among the assumptions confronted in *Equality, the Third World and Economic Delusion* are the beliefs (so frequently and faithfully reiterated from the pulpit, at synods and conferences, in print and through the media) that the West has prospered at the Third World's expense, that Western aid is necessary for economic development, that large-scale investment is indispensable for economic progress and that rapid population growth spells economic disaster. Published in 1981, this book develops ideas put forward initially in *Dissent on Development*, published in 1976. Commenting on the earlier book, Harry G. Johnson, former editor of *Encounter*, said: 'It ought to be read carefully by those of both the nominal Right and the nominal Left who profess to base their desire to promote development on a concern for the humanity and dignity of man.' Professor Bauer's latest contribution to this discussion, *Reality and Rhetoric: Studies in the Economics of Development* (on some of which an essay in this collection is based) will be published in 1984.

WCC and the Third World

The stance of the World Council of Churches towards the problems of Third World development comes under scrutiny in *Amsterdam to Nairobi: The World Council of Churches and the Third World* by Ernest Lefever. Published in 1979 by the Ethics and Public Policy Center in Washington, the book charts the troubled progress of the WCC from the Amsterdam Assembly of 1948 to the Nairobi Assembly of 1975 and beyond, tracing its movement away from a largely Western democratic concept of political responsibility to a more radical ideology that by 1975 had come to embrace the concept and practice of liberation theology. Professor Lefever analyses the strong resemblances between this 'revolutionary' theology and Marxist diagnoses of and prescriptions for Third World ills, showing that the WCC's ambiguous attitude towards Marxism — a blend of infatuation and fear — stems from a profound confusion of ends and means. He suggests that the Marxists' claim to a clear-cut explanation of poverty and to simple answers has a powerful appeal to Westerners who feel guilty about their power and wealth, whereas genuine Christianity offers no easy solutions to poverty, injustice or the lack of freedom. He ends by proposing seven ways in which the WCC could become truer to the Christian faith and make a more responsible contribution to the search for justice and freedom in the political world. 'Readers of [this] essay can decide for themselves the extent to which bad sociology, bad theology, bad faith, and, yes, sin feed on one another and are to blame for what the WCC has been doing.' (From the foreword by George F. Will)

Christian socialism

There is no shortage of Christian literature on the shortcomings (real and alleged) of the capitalist system. The classic Christian socialist critique of capitalism in Western Europe remains R. H. Tawney's *Religion and the Rise of Capitalism*, first published in 1926 and reprinted by Merton Books in 1960. Similarly important is Temple. Temple's work is well known though often not carefully read, as Oddie and Miller show elsewhere in this volume. *Christianity and the Social Order* (Shepheard-Walwyn-SPCK 1976) is probably the most significant.

Nearly fifty years after Tawney and Temple's powerful and influential presentation of the case for Christian socialism, the Bishop of Winchester, John V. Taylor, made his own eloquent statement of the case for a 'theology of enough' in the SCM publication, *Enough is Enough*. The date of publication (1975) is unfortunately reflected in the book's heavy reliance in its early chapters on the anti-growth arguments of the mid-seventies (such as those popularized by the Club of Rome), which have now been largely discredited. Two years later, Ronald Sider's *Rich Christians in an Age of Hunger* (Hodder & Stoughton) caused a considerable stir in evangelical circles with its analysis of world poverty (based on the thesis that the wealth of the rich countries has been gained at the expense of the exploited poor), and its call for a simpler lifestyle to implement biblical principles concerning poverty and possessions and for political action to remedy the structural evil underlying world hunger. *Bias to the Poor*, the latest contribution to this body of literature by another bishop, David Sheppard, has been subjected to rigorous criticism elsewhere in this volume. One chapter however — on the 'crisis of capitalism' — is particularly interesting as an attempt by a churchman in the Christian socialist tradition to analyze the Christian case for liberal capitalism. Not surprisingly, he finds the arguments wanting but his reaffirmation of the importance and goodness of wealth creation marks something of a departure from the almost exclusive emphasis on wealth redistribution that generally characterizes such critiques of the capitalist system. This does not, however, prevent him from proposing an international taxation system to reduce the disparity in income of the rich and poor countries of the world — one is left to imagine exactly how such a scheme might be implemented and with what political and economic consequences.

Capitalism and progress

Less well known than any of these is a book by the former Dutch MP, Bob Goudzwaard, now Professor of Economic Theory at the Free University of Amsterdam. *Capitalism and Progress: A Diagnosis of Western Society,* published in 1979 by the Wedge Publishing Foundation, examines the development of capitalism and its impact on Western culture. Ultimate responsibility for the Western world's current social and economic problems is attributed to what Goudzwaard regards as one of capitalism's most cherished articles of faith: the belief that human progress is a major objective of social life. He traces the consequences of this assumption from the Renaissance and Enlightenment periods to the present, arguing that a dedication to progress has not only failed to solve these problems but has served to compound them. Instead of further reliance on economic growth or scientific and technical advance, he urges a return to God-given norms of economy, technology, justice and morality which he regards as the only way to open up and unshackle 'a society which has become entangled in the toils of obedience to the autonomous forces of progress'.

The market and wealth creation

Two books by Professor Brian Griffiths see the relationship between Christianity and the market economy in more positive terms. A series of lectures given at the London Institute of Contemporary Christianity forms the basis of *Morality and the Market Place: Christian Alternatives to Capitalism and Socialism,* published in 1983 by Hodder & Stoughton. The first lecture locates the origin of the contemporary crisis of capitalism experienced both by the West and the Third World in the system's loss of legitimacy. The Christian values which once underpinned the market economy have been replaced by a rational humanism which fails to place adequate restraints on the exercise of freedom and which cannot generate a sufficiently strong sense of individual responsibility and human dignity to enable the market to function efficiently and with equity. The next lecture suggests that Marxism too is fatally flawed — it is economically inefficient and its implementation has brought in its wake religious persecution and political terror. Professor Griffiths argues that the basic problem with capitalist and Marxist ideologies alike is that they are both the products of the eighteenth-century Enlightenment, and despite their divergent emphases on freedom and control they are similarly imbued with the false values of secular humanism. He defends the positive benefits of a market economy, insisting however that it has to be bounded by Christian principles of justice derived from a biblical world view — there can be no market place without morality. Finally, he examines First World responsibility for the poor of the Third World, challenging the thesis that the rich owe their wealth to the exploitation of the poor and emphasizing the crucial importance of cultural factors in social and economic development. In *The Creation of Wealth*, to be published in 1984 by Hodder & Stoughton, Professor Griffiths explores four dimensions of wealth creation: the economic, theological, ethical and ideological, concluding that there are good economic, theological and moral reasons for valuing the market economy: for the Christian the challenge is to rescue the market economy from the stranglehold of humanistic capitalist ideology and to incorporate its positive features within a distinctively Christian framework. At a practical level, the business community is challenged to seek renewal not in the fashionable adoption of Japanese-style Buddhist or Confucian management principles but by once again espousing the Judaeo-Christian values of service, stewardship, community and justice under God.

Another advocate of the market economy within a Christian framework is Sir Fred Catherwood. His book, *The Christian in Industrial Society*, first published in 1964 and now something of a Christian classic, seeks to apply Christian principles to political, social and economic behaviour in the contemporary world. Among the topics covered are Christian attitudes to wealth and work, the social responsibility of big business and trades unions, the authority of government and the power of the shop floor, fair trading, making money on the Stock Exchange, and the Christian as employer and employee. The revised and enlarged edition of the book, published in 1980 by IVP, extends its scope to include such new developments as cost-push inflation, silicon-chip technology, mass unemployment and the black economy.

Economic systems and Christianity

One would be hard put to find a more concise critical survey of the main ideological frameworks for economic life advocated by Christians of varying political persuasions than J. Philip Wogaman's *Christians and the Great Economic Debate*, published in 1977 by the SCM Press. In this book, Marxism, laissez-faire capitalism, social market capitalism, democratic socialism and economic conservatism ('small is beautiful') are each examined for their compatibility with Christian moral imperatives and for their adequacy in dealing with the practical economic and social problems of the real world. Wogaman concludes that both Marxian Communism and laissez-faire capitalism have fatal flaws that would prevent Christians from espousing them without serious reservations, whereas the other three are each potentially receptive to most of the values that should claim the allegiance of Christians. He stresses the need for a dialogue between the advocates of each of these alternative approaches, particularly with regard to questions of economic and political power, the possibilities and limitations of human nature and the possibilities and limits of the natural world.

Ethics

Finally in this section, are three books dealing primarily with the ethical dimension of economic philosophy and policy-making. In 1971, Longmans, in association with the Institute of Economic Affairs, published H. B. Acton's essay in moral philosophy, *The Morals of Markets*. This 'ethical exploration' examines the principal moral objections to the market system — the self-centred nature of the profit motive and the spirit of aggressive competition that characterizes the market place. An analysis of the egalitarian alternatives to the market leads Professor Acton to the conclusion that their much-vaunted moral superiority is of dubious validity and that a centrally-planned economy is 'bound to lead to the authoritarian imposition of a state-controlled morality'. The search for equality is the theme of Sir Keith Joseph and Jonathan Sumption's essay, *Equality*, published in 1979 by John Murray. They argue that the pursuit of equality is not only impractical and self-defeating but, pursued for its own sake, is morally objectionable, as the price of attaining equality would be the sterilizing of human enterprise and the undermining of human brotherhood. Their concern is not only with the strident egalitarian ideology of the extreme left but also with the more instinctive egalitarian sympathies of many people in the West who would be horrified at the practical consequences of the implementation of their ideas.

A refreshingly sane and humane discussion of the ethical issues involved in developing economic policies to deal with the problems of Third World poverty is found in Peter Berger's *Pyramids of Sacrifice: Political Ethics and Social Change*, published in 1974 by Allen Lane. The book takes its title from the great pyramid of Cholula in Mexico. Succeeding pre-Columbian peoples made Cholula the centre of their state and a place of pilgrimage. Each added new sanctuaries to those they had conquered, to build one gigantic pyramid and when the Spaniards had established their rule they buried the pyramid under a mountain of dust and built yet another church on top: a succession of theories and ideologies provided by intellectuals (priests), embodied in stone by the wielders of power (aristocracy), dominating generations of peasants (laymen) who provided both the labour and the sacrifice. 'Thus the pyramid at Cholula becomes a metaphor for the relationship between theory, practice and those without a choice.'

Professor Berger argues that both capitalist ideology based on the ideal of growth and socialist ideology based on the ideal of revolution must be debunked.

> The critics of capitalism are right when they reject policies that accept hunger today while promising affluence tomorrow . . . The critics of socialism are right when they reject policies that accept terror today on the promise of a humane order tomorrow.

Taking Brazil and China as respectively the Third World's largest capitalist and socialist experiments, he contends that in one morally crucial aspect these two apparently opposite models of development belong in the same category — both are based on a willingness to sacrifice at least one generation to the putative goals of the experiment. He insists that rejection of both the Brazilian and Chinese models is the starting point for any morally defensible policy of development. The most pressing needs are, he suggests, in terms of physical deprivation and suffering and therefore the most pressing moral imperative in policy-making must be a 'calculus of pain'. And because human beings have the right to live in a meaningful world, an assessment of the costs of policy must also refer to a 'calculus of meaning'.

Modernity, he claims, exacts a high price at the level of meaning for many people and those unwilling to pay it must be taken seriously and not dismissed as irrational or backward. Indeed, the viability of modern societies will largely depend on their capacity to respond to counter-modernizing influences by creating inter-mediate institutions that will bridge the gulf between the modern state and the mass of uprooted individuals typical of modern societies. This policy imperative, he maintains, cuts across the capitalist/socialist dichotomy. The book concludes with a call for a new approach to political ethics and social change that will bring together two attitudes usually kept separate — those of hard-nosed analysis and of utopian imagination. 'What this book is finally all about is just this — some first steps towards a *hard-nosed utopianism.*'

The Weber thesis

No bibliographical survey of material about Christianity and capitalism would be complete without mention of the seminal writings of Max Weber, which still exert such a powerful and controversial influence today. The obvious starting point for a study of Weber's ideas about religion and society is, of course, *The Protestant Ethic and the Spirit of Capitalism*, first published in English by Allen & Unwin in 1930 and reprinted in 1976. In this work, Weber sought to show that there were certain affinities between the modern capitalist economic system that developed in Western Europe and North America and the ethical values and psychological motivations engendered by certain forms of Protestantism, particularly Calvinism. Weber also wrote three other less well known but nonetheless important works on the relationship between economic development and various non-Christian cultures: *The Religion of China*, which examines Confucianism and Taoism; *The Religion of India*, which explores the sociology of Hinduism and Buddhism; and *Ancient Judaism*, all published by The Free Press (in 1957, 1958 and 1952 respectively).

The importance of Weber's ideas is matched only by the confusion that now surrounds his thesis, both in terms of its validity and of what he actually meant. There is also a rather alarming tendency for many sociologists and anthropologists to evoke Weber's thesis with unwarranted alacrity to explain their data, although few would go as far as the American professor of economics, E. L. Hebden Taylor, who proclaimed in his recent book on *Economics, Money and Banking: Christian Principles* (Craig Press 1978) that since Max Weber had made it clear that Christianity instigated modernization in Europe, then 'a nation or a people [that] wishes to become modern . . . must "get" with Jesus Christ . . . for He is the great Modernizer of world history and . . . alone . . . the true source of all modernization and progress.' From here it is but a short step to his conclusion that development and modernization depend upon the formula: Resources plus Biblical Religion divided by Population equals Index of Standard of Living.

From such crude distortions of Weber's extremely subtle and sophisticated thesis, one turns with relief to two recently published commentaries on Weber and his ideas: Frank Parkin's *Max Weber* in the Key Sociologists Series, published by Ellis Harwood and Tavistock Publications in 1982; and Gordon Marshall's *In Search of the Spirit of Capitalism*, published by Hutchinson in the same year. Also by Gordon Marshall is the Clarendon Press publication *Presbyteries and Profits: Calvinism and the Development of Capitalism in Scotland, 1560-1707*. Published in 1980, it presents one of the best cases so far made in defence of the application of the Protestant ethic thesis to a particular society's economic development.

The Weber thesis and the Third World

It is however to the work of a Canadian anthropologist, Stanley Barrett, that one must look for a discussion — quite remarkable for its rigorous, honest and intelligent argument — of the application of the Weber thesis in a Third World context. *The Rise and Fall of an African Utopia* is the somewhat obscure title given to his brilliant analysis of the reasons for the extraordinary economic success of a small West African religious community called Olowo. As suggested by the sub-title — *A Wealthy Theocracy in Comparative Perspective* — this study (published in 1977 by Wilfred Laurier University Press) explores not only the ramifications of the Protestant ethic thesis as it has been applied to the larger Nigerian religious grouping of which the Olowo community is part, but also examines some of the main lines of argument in the wider Weberian debate, including McClelland's achievement thesis, Bellah's interpretation of the Japanese Bushido ethic as functionally equivalent to the Protestant ethic, and various attempts to test the validity of Weber's thesis in the context of such diverse communities as the Mourides of Senegal, the Giriama of Kenya, the Mennonites and Hutterites in Europe, and the Israeli kibbutzim. Although he concludes that the key factor in the Olowo community's sustained economic development was probably the motivation and social cohesion provided by the people's strong religious beliefs, he refuses the temptation (that has all too often proved irresistible to lesser scholars) to subsume his case study within the Weberian framework.

In place of the sloppy reasoning encountered with unwelcome frequency in writings on the vexed question of the relationship between economic development and culture, Barrett presents a closely reasoned argument in which he concludes that:

> What the Olowo case suggests is that most belief systems may contribute to development if properly utilised . . . The effect that Olowo's religious beliefs had on the economy was nothing short of astounding. If they could perform as they did without being in any way unusually suited for the job, I would think that most belief systems could do the same thing, given the proper circumstances.

The implications for those concerned with development is that the need is 'not so much to destroy what might stand in the way, but to build on what is there, and to supplant existing arrangements where necessary'. At this point we are a long way indeed from Hebden Taylor's prescription for economic development — the revolutionary overthrow of traditional culture systems and their replacement with a thoroughly Westernized form of Christianity.

Anthropological and sociological studies

A number of other anthropological and sociological studies explore the relationships between culture and economic life. In *Politics, Personality and Nation-Building* (Massachusetts Institute of Technology 1962), Lucien Pye attempts to explain the failure of development in Burma in terms of the absence of certain values such as security, trust and decisiveness, which are crucial to development. Cultural factors are also emphasized in Edward Banfield's *The Moral Basis of a Backward Society*, published by The Free Press in 1958. He argues that the extreme poverty of the village he studied in South Italy could be attributed to the inability of the villagers to act together for their own good or for any end transcending the short-term material interest of the nuclear family. This barrier to political and economic progress is seen to be the consequence of an ethos which Banfield designates 'amoral familism' and which he sees as indicative of the crucial importance of culture in determining the level of organization and therefore of economic development in a society.

In *Tzintzuntzan: Mexican Peasants in a Changing World*, the American anthropologist G. M. Foster shows how the perception of wealth as something fixed has discouraged self-improvement and progress. Turning to Africa, an extremely well-researched book by Adda Bozeman, entitled *Conflict in Africa* and published by the Princeton University Press in 1976, offers a remarkable insight into the 'shared cultural realities' of Africa south of the Sahara, in particular the distinctive features of societies characterized for centuries by non-literate patterns of thought and communication and consequently shaped by a mythical vision of history and society.

Islamic culture and its relation to economic life is the focus of the French sociologist Maxime Rodinson's famous study *Islam and Capitalism*, first published in French in 1966 and published in English by Penguin in 1974. In this book, Rodinson analyses the social and economic development of Islamic countries to discern how the precepts of the Muslim religion — mutual aid, respect for property, equality before God, the prohibition of profits — could affect capitalist development, and he assesses the extent to which exhortations to justice, charity and co-operation have inclined the Muslim world towards socialism. Also from Penguin is V. S. Naipaul's deservedly popular *Among the Believers*, published in 1981. This fascinating and highly readable account of a journey through the cultural world of Islamic fundamentalism in Iran, Pakistan, Malaysia and Indonesia, yields valuable insights into the economic implications of the contemporary revival of traditional Muslim cultural values in these countries. Two more books by the same author explore the cultural world of India. *An Area of Darkness*, published in 1964, is a reflective and semi-autobiographical account of a year in India; although of Indian extraction himself, he finds many aspects of Hindu culture strangely alien. *India: A Wounded Civilization* (1977) is an extended study of Indian attitudes, prompted by the 1975 Emergency.

In *The Third World Calamity*, published by Routledge & Kegan Paul in 1981, the journalist Brian May uses material gathered from Iran, India and Nigeria to argue his case that economic development in these Third World countries is blocked by the same cultural inertia that previously made Africa and Asia vulnerable to imperialism. Because of this, it is only a small, Westernized élite that has tended to prosper materially from Western-style economic expansion. He seeks to elucidate the psychological factors that he sees as part of the explanation for the contrast between European dynamism and the stagnation of Africa and Asia at the onset of the colonial period. Citing the Iranian experience, he demonstrates that the superficial imposition of Western-inspired socio-economic structures on people with an utterly different cultural background, rarely succeeds. He ends with a plea for greater recognition of the cultural barriers to development, so that the West may avoid doomed attempts at economic expansion and the inhabitants of Africa and Asia might be spared some of the disastrous social dislocation presently being inflicted upon them.

English culture and the industrial spirit

Returning finally to our own society, Martin Wiener's *English Culture and the Decline of the Industrial Spirit, 1850-1980*, published in 1981 by the Cambridge University Press, is a mine of sources culled from a wide range of nineteenth- and twentieth-century English writings, illustrating a general cultural disdain for the values and achievements of industrial capitalism. Professor Wiener shows how during the Victorian era the dynamic and enterprising 'workshop of the world' became an increasingly conservative society, dominated by a middle-class élite educated in the attitudes and values of a pseudo-aristocratic culture that was hostile to economic development. He argues that these anti-industrial and anti-business attitudes have had important consequences for British industry, as innovation has been stymied and production processes allowed to become antiquated and inefficient. Britain's present economic malaise, he believes, has its roots deep in the social and mental structures of the nation. On his reckoning, calls for economic revitalization must be reviewed in the light of more than a hundred years of cultural animosity towards economic growth — often an uncomprehending hostility that has spanned the political divide and sunk deep roots into the hearts more than the minds of many in the Church.

15

Eating Sheppard's Pie:
Hints on Reading the Sociological Gospel

Digby Anderson

Taking Church reports 'seriously'

You will usually find it in the 'Foreword' of a church report, and often in the final paragraph. Just before the author of the foreword appends his, overwhelmingly, episcopal signature, he will commend the report for discussion: 'I am happy to commend it for widespread study and discussion.'[1] Sometimes a precise audience is indicated: 'I commend this report to the serious consideration of the General Synod.'[2] Sometimes authors are a little more reckless about the response they invite: ' . . . it is worthy of the committed attention of the churches.'[3] It may be Christians, churchpeople, Catholics or the members of one of the many committees which adorn the modern Church who are addressed. They may be 'invited', 'urged', chided or even obliged to read the report. And afterwards they might 'be better informed', 'discuss', 'debate' rather more energetically, 'draw up a plan of action' or numinously 'respond'.

The topics of these reports vary but I shall mainly consider those which discuss social issues such as overseas aid, unemployment, health or housing. Perhaps less obviously sociological than these, are publications which have a sociological component, for example, technical arguments about how to increase liturgical 'participation', and theological texts which make sociological assumptions about the wishes and capabilities of 'modern man', 'man-come-of-age' or 'secularized man'. I shall consider these more briefly.

How should churchpeople, both priests and laity, respond to this new mandatum to read and discuss reports and books. More precisely, how should they read the sociological parts of such reports? Foreword writers are not given to wanton explicitness, and the nearest we get to an answer is the request to read 'seriously'. This is unreasonable. It should be rephrased at least to 'be willing or prepared to consider reading them seriously'. The reports are a very mixed bag indeed, some are careful, well researched and important; others particularly sections of *Development Education*[4] or *The Cuts and the Wounds*,[5] tendentious and trivial. The prospect of the myriad committees of the Church abusing their God-given time 'considering' these latter reports 'seriously' is worrying. Although 'serious consideration' sounds a modest enough 'response' to request, a little thought shows that 'seriousness' is not to be indulged in promiscuously and accorded to everything upon demand. Sometimes the reactions will be hilarity, amazement or contempt. On occasions these will not be only permissible responses for the lighthearted, but more appropriate responses than 'seriousness' because they will be the responses which fit the character of the report.

More than a century ago, biblical scholars were urged to treat their text as a book like any other. It was a silly suggestion for books differ, but it contained the useful idea that we should look at the character of a text before deciding the criteria on which to judge it. What is the character of the reports? First, and most obvious, they are mixtures, mixtures of doctrine, official figures of social issues, appeals to sentiment, sociological concepts, careful argument and ideology. They are hotchpotches, stews and pies. Second, they use their sources selectively. Because they are hotchpotches, their sociological ingredients are very much bits and pieces of borrowed wisdom and can all too easily be yesterday's sociological meat, left-over, minced and reheated. Third, some of the wisdom was not very good in the first place. The idea that mixtures, composed dishes, can get away with inferior meat is an English nonsense. If yesterday's meat was poor yesterday served on its own, it will not be better today as the basis of a pie. Poorly warmed up, it threatens indiscriminate consumers with the cognitive equivalent of salmonella poisoning.

Three questions

There are three sets of questions a serious reader of a sociologically informed church report might ask:

How does the report achieve any impact it has? What are the *main* ingredients of the argument? Most arguments will be a mixture with, for example, statistics and appeals to sentiment, but is the basis of the argument fact or sentiment? Also, how are the ingredients of the argument blended together? Is the sauce used to disguise poor quality ingredients or even to make it difficult to discern the meat from the other ingredients?

Does the author borrow facts, concepts and arguments from other studies in an explicit and methodical way? Or does he just use up what is in the nearest larder?

Were the facts, concepts and arguments of good quality and reputation in their original (sociological) discipline? Has he borrowed prime beef or indigestible gristle?

How does the report achieve its impact?

Consider, initially, *Development Education* (1983)[6] because it is a very good example of the *rhetoric* of 'debate'. In several places it describes itself as enabling churchpeople to 'think' about its 'fight for world development', and it claims to want 'a new under-standing of *poverty* and its *causes* and *consequences* both in our own society and in the Third World'. This invitation to 'think' is also implied on the cover through the title. It is an educational exercise called 'Development Education'. In fact it is difficult to think of a less educational document than *Development Education*. It appears unprepared to *think* about development at all. It accepts uncritically the much-criticized Brandt Report, quoting it throughout as authority. It glibly accepts the thorny concept of corporate sin without any discussion. Its 'information' section is not purely informational. It refers only to those biblical texts which reinforce its own understanding of poverty and justice. It ignores published analysis of development problems which diverges from its own. And it is so confident it knows the answers that it adopts a most uneducational tone, 'Why do we engage in the struggle?'

Development Education is not about education at all. It is propaganda determined to *disseminate* a particular viewpoint. The point is not that this viewpoint is wrong or right but that 'serious' reading of the report shows that it is not the sort of report it claims to be. Even a tendentious report such as *Development Education* could have been properly educational if

159

balancing reports had been made available or at least referred to. Debate assumes sides, at least two of them.

The juxtaposition of a declared wish to learn with an apparent predisposition to judgement is even more pronounced in another report, the *World Council of Churches Programme on Transnational Corporations*.[7] Its authors deserve credit for accomplishing this dramatic juxtaposition within one sentence. The sentence starts declaring their aim to explore and to question the issue of TNCs and then shows immediately that exploring and questioning are the last things they are prepared to do: 'The aim was to explore and question the issue of TNCs from a position of solidarity with the victims of TNC operations' (p. 2).

A recent public reading of excerpts from this report at the Institute of Economic Affairs had an audience of economists — not the most jocular of scholars — in convulsions of laughter. This seems a far more appropriate, and hence 'serious' reaction to it than extended discussion in church committee. But the economists laughed because they knew the report was tendentious. They had read alternative studies. Have the church committees? A careful reading of *Development Education* and the WCC report shows that any impact they have, derives not from carefully marshalled and analysed facts but a sentimental rhetoric of compassion (not an ethic, a rhetoric), a frantic exhortation to action, the invocation of dramatic dualisms and Marxist demon-ology and an appeal to (corporate) guilt and political and bureaucratic activism. It is important to realize that these qualities may make a text more not less attractive, at least on a superficial reading. One object of serious reading is to examine critically documents which are initially attractive.

There are many ways in which ideas can be attractive, at least to some people, without necessarily being true, sound or practical. David Sheppard's *Bias to the Poor*[8] contains many examples. Its overall sympathetic impact comes, I think, from two sources. First the book allows us to paint a picture of the author both by his direct and indirect self-reference. The reader builds up a picture of the Bishop of Liverpool as a man who is committed to helping the poor, and convinced of the scriptural imperative to do so. The book is sympathetic because the author is. Secondly the book persistently appeals to a state of affairs which we feel 'ought' to be possible. Not for the Bishop a cool assessment of what existing strategies have to offer the poor but an exhortation to renewed commitment, to prophesy. And yet, it is not all exhortation. The book appears to have its feet on the ground, especially in some chapters which chronicle the Bishop's experiences or cite published research. Whatever the value of such an approach — now fact, now hope, now real possibility, now utopia — such ambivalence makes the book hard to assess. It is certainly not in the WCC camp, a candidate for hilarious convulsion. It certainly should be read but precisely because it is initially attractive and yet slippery, it should be read very critically.

David Sheppard's sentences seduce the reader and serious readers should beware. For example, talking about the poverty of the young people of Liverpool he writes, 'The poverty which the young people had seen and objected to, robbed the urban poor of any choices.'[9] He then goes on to build a substantial argument on this definition of poverty as no choice. Of course, it is simply untrue, especially when he keeps emphasizing that his definition of 'poverty' is *relative* to others who are better off. Such poverty does not rob the poor of *any* choices. People who are poor make many choices, some within their poverty and some escaping it. Equally certainly poverty makes some choices more difficult. There are two issues. First why has a statement so *palpably untrue* remained in a book of which the draft was read by five people mentioned in the preface including an Archdeacon and a Roman Catholic Bishop plus proof readers and editors? Is it because, however untrue it may be, it sounds as if it ought to be true?

Second, once we admit that it is untrue the business becomes much more complicated. Poverty restricts some choices: Which ones? How much? In what circumstances? Riches also restrict choices, not as much, but how and when? When David Sheppard defines an important choice as concerned with 'decisions . . . which affect our lives' or taking 'part in that network',[10] what would satisfy him as participation? This is not the tedious sociologist saying it is all more complicated. The crucial point is that once it is expressed in a 'more complicated' way, the rhetoric collapses. Another less crucial example, 'Christians should take a lead in a public campaign to challenge the assumption that everyone pays their taxes grudgingly and unwillingly. Taxation is a proper way by which wealth is distributed more fairly and by which the poor and the whole of society are given better opportunities.'[11]

One small change would make this excerpt quite acceptable though less forceful. Taxation 'is' not what Sheppard suggests it is. Perhaps it 'should be'. But there we have it, the slippery slope between description and exhortation. Apparently the Bishop has his feet on the ground but in truth he is airborne. As description the statement is nonsense. Obviously *if* tax is redistributive it cannot give the 'whole' of society more opportunities; most, possibly, but not all, unless something rather unusual is meant by better opportunities. Then again questions are begged in the use of the term 'fair' to describe income redistributed by politicians. Last there is an open question about whether tax works as Sheppard suggests. Many welfare benefits are rendered in the form of services and the (middle-class) service producers benefit from them. There is an argument over the extent to which taxes are finally redistributive in the way Sheppard implies. Is taxing those who earn as little as £40 a week to subsidize middle-class children with free university education fair? Again the issue is not about taxation per se but the need for readers of such books as *Bias to the Poor* to remain serious, and unseduced.

Borrowing from sociology

The first question we asked is a practical proposition for many readers. It amounts to little more than reading church reports on social issues carefully and critically, asking if they are what they say they are, looking for both sides of a controversy to be explained or at least referred to, and asking ourselves what it was in the report that gave it any impact it had.

The second question is: Does the author borrow facts, concepts and arguments from sociological studies in a methodical way? It is rather more difficult to answer. Many church reports refer to facts, concepts or arguments established in some other document, a document to which many readers will not have access. One can see why church reports do this. A small fraction of their audience may find it useful and it is part of the business of producing 'professional' reports. Yet, while ordinary readers cannot be expected to extend their 'serious' reading to sources, they can at least look to see how the sources are used.

Readers should expect to find facts such as official statistics in reports, but they should also expect a note explaining the pitfalls with using any *particular* set of figures. They should be cautious of any report which treats the figures as if they have one and only one clear policy implication. They should also be careful of reports in which the evidence is mixed up with the conclusions so as to make it difficult to read off any different conclusion from the data. It will not always be possible for report writers to have clear sections termed evidence, analysis and conclusions and one would not necessarily wish it, but one would be suspicious of the sort of report that so enmeshed these that it pushed all thoughts towards one conclusion. Perhaps one way of expressing this is that a good report will not be too 'tidy'.

Consider as an example 'The Cuts and the Wounds'[12] sections of which are an appalling presentation of 'facts' about reductions in welfare expenditure. Nowhere is there an *adequate* discussion of the level of cuts and the difficulties of establishing such levels. Nowhere is there a consideration of whether the cuts in state sectors, which are much less than the economies in the private sector, are really vicious. Reductions in services are juxtaposed with reductions in spending by central government as though the latter led directly and inevitably to the former. The evidence is just not presented in such a way as to allow any judgement on the extent to which welfare employees have preserved their jobs at the expense of clients' services. It does not permit an assessment of whether there is any slack in public services which could be taken up without reducing consumer satisfaction. It displays no interest in whether bureaucrats have administered the cuts well or whether previous levels of funding were justified.

This pamphlet also teaches the reader to judge a text by what it does, not what it says. The authors certainly proclaim that the statistics are difficult to interpret, especially those about relative incomes. But this does not actually make them careful in using such figures. Six lines after bewailing the difficulties, they are advocating democratization (equalization?) of incomes.

But church books and pamphlets do not only borrow statistics from social science sources. They borrow concepts. Running through *Bias to the Poor* is the concept of relative poverty, elaborated to a fine art by Peter Townsend in *Poverty in the UK*.[13] I am poor because I have less than you. Poverty hurts

163

because I know you have more than I. Poverty is having less than what is accepted as normal, a changing amount. Poverty is exclusion from normal goods and chances. This is not the place to criticize relativist concepts of poverty but to note two qualifications. First, they have been criticized, and even by those who sympathize with them.[14] Sheppard manages to make relative poverty the cornerstone of his book without once describing and addressing such criticisms. That is an example of borrowing a concept in an unmethodical way.

Second, the attempt to make poverty relative is an example of sociological corsetry whereby a familiar sympathetic concept has its contours subtly changed and distorted so as to include new recipients of compassion. Poverty is untied from lack of subsistence resources and stitched up to inequality. Its cure is not now the supply of basic needs but egalitarianism. And the means of that supply is political and collectivist. Relative poverty swells the number of the poor. It makes poverty something ineradicable this side of the Marxist revolution. The poor cease to be marginal and become identified with the general working class. It can even be argued that such a view distracts attention from the really poor. The Church has a long tradition of speaking about the poor and truly caring for them. One would have expected more care in referring to them from one of its bishops. At least he might have shown himself aware of the difficulties.

Bias to the Poor is 252 pages long but nowhere in it is there discussion of the three concepts that underpin it, (relative) poverty, unemployment and racism. What I have been arguing is that when a writer such as David Sheppard makes such extensive and crucial use of so vague a concept, the reader might expect a brief discussion of why that concept was chosen, why that and not another, and what the problems are with it. Sociology and economics are not disciplines to be pillaged for bits and pieces which might be useful. Or rather, authors *may* pillage them and often do in the name of interest and education: 'I want to look at the problem from the perspective of . . .', or 'Let's define poverty in a relative way and . . .' They are at liberty to do so: but then so is the reader at liberty to say, 'No, let's not.'

Let us be quite clear that my primary aim is not to criticize *Bias to the Poor* or to suggest that its author should write differently. The concern of this chapter is with the *reader* and the sort of obligation he is under when such books are commended to him. There is a feeling that if a book or report is about the poor and the needy then we, members of a Church which cares for the poor, should take it seriously. I have suggested that this will depend not only on the poor and our care for them but on the character of the book. David Sheppard has done a service in reminding us of our obligation to the poor but that does not mean his analysis is worth taking seriously. Indeed, his contribution may even be damaging unless it provokes readers to question the conclusions he asserts.

How good was the sociological discipline?

We now move from the use authors of church reports make of 'sociological' sources to the sources themselves. There is, of course, no reason why church documents should include sociological arguments, but if they are to do so it is important that they are clear about the nature of the discipline they are using. It may be that sociology and sociological sources can be of service to the Church in her concerns and that they solve some problems. But they also bring with them a new set of problems. It does seem as if the Church is sometimes rather envious of other disciplines, imagining that they have the answers to problems its own traditional approaches find difficult. Successively, it has seized on psycho-analysis (via clinical theology), community work and Marxism (via liberation theology) in the hope that these will provide answers. Answers of course they may help to provide, but they also throw up new sets of problems.

None of the reports I have considered *explicitly declares* that there are no problems in the use of sociological arguments. We do not find explanations prefaced by, 'Sociologists are agreed that . . .', or, 'It is a sociological fact that . . .', or 'Sociological studies have established that . . .'. The nearest we get is the claim that a study has 'shown that . . .' followed by a reference. As Sharrock has pointed out,[15] sociologists themselves are prone to this sort of inflation claiming that they have 'shown' something to be the case when they have only argued it to be the case. But if the report writers do not *declare* their uncritical confidence in sociological unanimity or finality they do *imply* it. Consider the way that the Bishop uses a particular study to make statements about divisions in the working class. Now the *Affluent Worker in Class Structure* is certainly not a bad study. It is indeed a very famous study, but it was conducted fifteen to twenty years ago. It is not about the working class but a rather peculiar section of it, high-earning car workers in a boom town (Luton) in the sixties, and it has, naturally, been subject to considerable criticism since. Further, sociological studies become famous and, more important, continue to be famous and taught for all sorts of reasons: they may be 'interesting', a good example of one kind of approach, methodologically important, or the first of their kind. Fame does not necessarily imply enduring truth. To say then that the *Affluent Worker* is a good or a famous study does not mean it is available, without more ado, as a reliable way of classifying half the population. David Sheppard, in particular, makes his reference to sociological arguments almost with no introduction at all in the text, and nearly all his notes are not notes at all but simple bare references. If he is critically aware of the sort of discipline he is using, he does not bother to show it. What *is* that discipline like?

What I shall term social-issue-sociology has five characteristics which readers should take into account when reading church reports that in some measure rely on it. First much of it is *predisposed* to look for explanations at a high level of generality. It investigates the relation between, say, crime and social class or youth or even a particular youth culture. It does not look for individualistic (moral) explanations and thus does not, often, produce them. Related to this is a sociological tendency to talk as if human events happen without human agency. David Sheppard falls into this habit, talking, for example, of rates 'falling' on people. Sociology does not displace moral explanation. Its emphasis on factors outside the individual is the result of its own preferred methods. It should not then be used to show that, for example, crime is caused by social factors *rather than* moral factors or to *reduce* individual responsibility for crimes. Call this the characteristic of *predisposition*.

Second, though such sociology (and I include in it social policy) contains conclusions, analysis and evidence, it should not be assumed that the evidence *dictates* the analysis or that the conclusion reached in any study is the only possible conclusion. One can say of a good study that its conclusions are consistent with its data and often little more. Each sociologist chooses how to analyse and argue from his data and often different conclusions are consistent with the same evidence. This is even more the case when policy implications are drawn. If a series of attempts to engineer better job chances for working class children by comprehensivization, mixed ability and expanded higher education appear to have failed, what do we decide? That such interventions were mistaken and should be reversed or that they were insufficient and should be extended? Do the agreed errors of mass housing justify giving private contractors more or less freedom? Call this the characteristic of *data indeterminacy*. I am not suggesting that further evidence may not be brought that might help to direct the answer a little one way or the other, but that readers should have realistic assessments about the degree of finality such sociology can offer.

The third characteristic springs from this 'data indeterminacy'. Sociologists disagree. More than that, they disagree a lot. Disagreement is of course a method of science, and not a bad thing, but users of sociology should be aware of just how much disagreement exists in sociology about what the facts are, and what good analysis is, as well as about conclusions. Such disagreements are fuelled by sociology's tendency to fashion. Why, for example, is the invocation of greater sexual equality so popular *now* — surely not because sex differences are more extreme! And the disagreement is often politicized. Call this characteristic *controversy*.

Fourth, sociology is partly a scientific and partly a literary discipline. Its arguments impress partly because of evidence, but also partly because of the way they are presented. It is deeply *rhetorical*. Sociology's words are often everyday words such as 'poverty' 'class' and 'alienation' with heightened and adapted meaning. They carry associations which no amount of 'cold' presentation can avoid. Sometimes it is the rhetoric which sways readers. Running through much social policy is a vocabulary of 'care', 'community', and 'need', which is highly seductive and which the Church is currently, increasingly and tediously repeating. 'Care-share-speak' is no substitute for analysis nor does bewailing need do duty for efficient response. Indeed it is often used to justify inefficient responses.

To these four characteristics — a predisposition to some sorts of explanations, data indeterminacy, controversy and rhetoric — we should add a fifth, that sociology is coy and ambivalent about these very characteristics. Look at its publications, especially those of the early seventies, and you will find sociologists of social issues themselves expressing strong doubts about the adequacy of their discipline. Such doubts are less vocal now, not because they have been resolved, but because many sociologists feel that in order to protect the discipline in a climate of academic retrenchment it is better to show a confidence in one's discipline's conclusions and usefulness.

What do these characteristics add up to? Certainly sociology is a discipline which can be thoughtful, fascinating and educational, but it is rarely a discipline capable of furnishing ready, final and agreed analyses of social issues; it is helpful in depicting social trends but inclined to social indictment and poor as a basis for scientific social engineering. The reader of the church report need not bother himself with the details. He need only have a very general image. For his concern is whether the authors of reports which use such sociology *show* an awareness of the materials they are using. There is little in publications I have discussed that shows such an awareness.

Conclusion

There are then three fairly simple ways of reading a church report which make use of what I have called social-issue-sociology.

Read the text carefully looking for the pitfalls indicated above.

Ask if it uses its sources in a clear and methodical way.

Ask if it *shows* an awareness of the general character of the discipline it relies on.

Our discussion has centred on church sociologizing about social issues such as unemployment or poverty. But it should be briefly noted that the problem is wider than this. Modern theologians are increasingly making statements about 'man' which are ambivalent, being somewhat ontological — somewhat sociological. Ogden writes: '*The educated man of today* is . . . *typically* interested in . . . preserving a measure of personal authenticity against the pressures toward conformity of a technological civilisation',[16] or again of '*our typical experience* and thought as *secular men*',[17] or of '*modern man's* alleged "atheism"'.[18] Macquarrie writes of the 'alternative confronting *us*',[19] and Bultman of the 'words of the Bible which in their mythological form have become incomprehensible to the *man of today*'.[20] We ought to note two things about such statements. First they are cornerstones of contemporary theological argument. It is because today's man is alleged to have certain difficulties with traditional theologies and certain needs of new ones that much of the effort to create novel theologies and, to some extent, revised liturgies is excused. Second, some of the statements are, in part, sociological; they are statements about the cultural capacities and practices of men today.

Are men like this? Which men? Do men have these difficulties, these rather than other difficulties? Have any of these authors tried to find out? Or are they difficulties which theologians have and suppose that others ought to have? Surely here we have another abuse of sociology, if an abuse by neglect. Sociology *has* something to say about trends in secularization and it, together with anthropology and linguistics, has something to say about myths and symbols. What they have to say would not provide easy answers as with the case of social issues but it might stop the easy sociological suppositions that modern theologians are making and on which they base so much. There is room then for the Church, its theologians and its social gospellers to listen to and use sociological arguments but they should do so with more care than is often taken.

This chapter started by describing various church books and reports as stews or pies in which sociology, economics, theology, doctrine, ideology, appeals to sentiment, and careful arguments are blended together. Some of the stews I have discussed are not very successful. They blend the mixture in an unsatisfactory way and they do not appear to understand the sociological ingredient they use. But the fact that there are bad stews does not mean we should stop making stews — they can be nourishing dishes! Nor should churchpeople and committees stop reading and discussing these reports. They should, however, approach them with critical caution and, if appropriate, not hesitate to reject the poor ones with contempt, hilarity and speed.

NOTES

1   *Work and the Future*, A Report from the Industrial Committee of the General Synod Board for Social Responsibility (CIO 1979) Foreword.

2   *Housing and Homelessness*, A Report of the Social Policy Committee of the Board for Social Responsibility (CIO 1982) Foreword.

3   *The Cuts and the Wounds*, Report of the Internal Economy Group of the Thames North Province Church and Society Panel, 1982.

4   *Development Education for the Church of England*, Board for Social Responsibility. CIO 1983.

5   op. cit.

6   op. cit.

7   World Council of Churches Programme on Transnational Corporations Document 2.3, WCC Geneva, 1982.

8   D. Sheppard, *Bias to the Poor*. Hodder & Stoughton 1983.

9   ibid., p. 12.

10 ibid., p. 13.

11 ibid., pp. 133-4.

12 op. cit.

13 P. Townsend, *Poverty in the United Kingdom*. Penguin 1979.

14 John Gladwin, *Poverty in a World of Wealth, Shaft* No. 36, Autumn 1982.

15 W. W. Sharrock 'The Possibility of Social Change', in D. Anderson, ed., *The Ignorance of Social Intervention*. Croom Helm 1979.

16 S. Ogden, *The Reality of God* (Harper & Row 1963) p. 11.

17 ibid., p. 19.

18 ibid., p. 51.

19 J. Macquarrie, *Principles of Christian Theology* (SCM Review edn 1977) p. 73.

20 R. Bultman in *The Listener* (5 February 1983) pp. 217-18.

THE SOCIAL AFFAIRS UNIT

The Unit is a research and educational trust committed both to the promotion of lively and wide-ranging debate on social affairs and to the sociological analysis of key controversies in contemporary culture. Its immediate programme is the building of a systematic literature on the practical outcome of government attempts at social engineering in the fields of education, health, social welfare, discrimination and criminal rehabilitation. The Unit's work is assisted by an Advisory Council which includes:

Titles published by the Unit:

Tracts Beyond the Times
    Charles Elwell   £1.50
Are the Police Fair?
    Dr P. A. J. Waddington   £1.00
Are the Police Under Control?
    Professor David Regan   £1.00
Home Truths
    Malcolm Hoppe et al   £2.95
Detecting Bad Schools
    Dr Digby Anderson   £2.65
Educated for Employment?
    Professor David Marsland et al   £2.65
Pied Pipers of Education
    Professor Anthony Flew et al   £2.65
Criminal Welfare on Trial
    Dr Colin Brewer et al   £2.65
Breaking the Spell of the Welfare State
    Dr Digby Anderson et al   £2.65

Available from good bookshops or The Social Affairs Unit, 2 Lord North Street London S.W.1.

THE INSTITUTE OF ECONOMIC AFFAIRS

The Institute has published over 300 titles, of which the following are most relevant to the contents of this book: